First World War

and Army of Occupation

War Diary

France, Belgium and Germany

5 CAVALRY DIVISION
Headquarters, Branches and Services
Royal Army Veterinary Corps
Assistant Director Veterinary Services
1 January 1917 - 30 January 1918

WO95/1162/5

The Naval & Military Press Ltd
www.nmarchive.com
Published in association with The National Archives

Published by

The Naval & Military Press Ltd

Unit 10 Ridgewood Industrial Park,

Uckfield, East Sussex,

TN22 5QE England

Tel: +44 (0) 1825 749494

www.naval-military-press.com

www.nmarchive.com

This diary has been reprinted in facsimile from the original. Any imperfections are inevitably reproduced and the quality may fall short of modern type and cartographic standards.

Contents

WO 95/1162/5

1917-1918

5TH CAVALRY DIVISION

ASST DIR. VETY SERVICES

~~JAN 1917~~ SEPT - JAN 1918

Instructions regarding War Diaries and Intelligence Summaries are contained in F. S. Regs., Part II. and the Staff Manual respectively. Title pages will be prepared in manuscript.

WAR DIARY
or
INTELLIGENCE SUMMARY.
(Erase heading not required.)

Vol VII

Army Form C. 2118.

A.D.V.S. 5th Cavalry Division

Place	Date	Hour	Summary of Events and Information	Remarks and references to Appendices
	1.1.17		Made arrangements with G.O.C. Secunderabad & Canadian Cavalry Brigade for elementary Veterinary demonstration to junior officers & senior N.C.O. of units	
	2.1.17		Arranged veterinary demonstration for junior officers & senior N.C.O. with G.O.C. Ambala Cavalry Bde. Inspected R.H.A. Brigade, Ammunition Column & X Battery R.H.A. Discovered bad outbreak of mange in X Battery	
	3.1.17		G.O.C. inspected horses of Divisional Headquarters. Inspected Auxiliary Horse Transport & Reserve Park with Veterinary Officer i/c.	
	4.1.17		General inspection of X Battery R.H.A. found 19 cases of mange & whole rest in contact with mange cases. Made arrangements for treating mange cases in lines. Gave lecture to officers & N.C.Os R.C.H.A. on Mange	
	5.1.17		M.V.S. Ambala Brigade inspection, Diagnosis of mange in X Battery confirmed. Arrangements for local treatment	
	6.1.17		Inspected M.V.S. Lucknow Cavalry Bde & saw [illegible] cases.	
	7.1.17		D.D.V.S. Cavalry Corps inspected conditions for treating mange in R.H.A.	
	9.1.17		Inspected mange treatment at X Battery. Conditions most favourable.	
	10.1.17		Inspected M.V.S. Canadian Cavalry Brigade saw [illegible] cases	

Instructions regarding War Diaries and Intelligence Summaries are contained in F. S. Regs., Part II. and the Staff Manual respectively. Title pages will be prepared in manuscript.

WAR DIARY
or
INTELLIGENCE SUMMARY.
(Erase heading not required.)

Army Form C. 2118.

Place	Date	Hour	Summary of Events and Information	Remarks and references to Appendices
	11.1.17		Inspected X Battery RHA. Re-sights of Mange. Horses improving.	
	12.1.17		Inspected MVS Ambala Brigade saw Mange [illegible] of Machine Gun Squadron. Inspected Ambala Machine Gun Squadron.	
	13.1.17		GOC inspected Auxiliary Horse Transport Coy & Reserve Park - Visited X Battery. Lieutenant T.G.E. GALLIE Rve. placed on sick list.	
	14.1.17		Inspected MVS Secunderabad. Saw [illegible] cases.	
	15.1.17		Inspected MVS Ambala Cavalry Bde. Saw Machine Gun [illegible] of Mange. Inspected Field Squadron R.E. evacuated 1 case Mange.	
	18.1.17		Inspected RCHA evacuated several cases of Mange especially from B Battery. Arranged treatment of [illegible] horses affected with Mange in areas occupied by British troops.	
	19.1.17		Inspected Auxiliary Horse Transport Coy & Reserve Park. Also Canadian Mobile Vety Section.	
	20.1.17		Inspected X Battery Mange cases. Lieutenant GALLIE rejoined from sick list.	
	21.1.17		Inspected for Mange RCHA found 21 cases Mange. Put [illegible] of treatment into working order. Arranged for supply of material & staff for dealing with Mange in Unit lines.	
	22.1.17		Went to No 5 Veterinary Hospital Abbeville.	
	23.1.17		DADVS Cavalry Corps cast horses for Remount reasons at HdQrs Canadian Cavalry Bde.	

Instructions regarding War Diaries and Intelligence Summaries are contained in F. S. Regs., Part II. and the Staff Manual respectively. Title pages will be prepared in manuscript.

WAR DIARY
or
INTELLIGENCE SUMMARY.

(Erase heading not required.)

Army Form C. 2118.

Place	Date	Hour	Summary of Events and Information	Remarks and references to Appendices
	23.1.17		Lieutenant GALLIE AVC [illegible] [illegible] applies for reinforcement	
	24.1.17		Inspected Canadian Machine Gun Squadron & [illegible], saw [illegible] [illegible] at M.V.S.	
	25.1.17		Saw [illegible] [illegible] [illegible] [illegible] & [illegible] of Mange.	
	26.1.17		Inspected Mange cases under treatment at RCHA [illegible] & Battery RHA	
	27.1.17		Inspected M.V.S. [illegible] & Regimental [illegible] of 9th Hodsons ~~Horse~~ Lieutenant GALLIE [illegible] to U.K. Capt F.W. MEDLOCK AVC arrives & [illegible] [illegible] [illegible] [illegible] [illegible] in place of Lieut GALLIE AVC.	
	29.1.17		Inspected M.V.S. Canadian Cavalry Bde & saw [illegible]	
	30.1.17		Inspected A Battery & [illegible] RCHA arranged [illegible] of [illegible] Mange cases Fort Garry Horse	
	31.1.17		Inspected [illegible] cases of Mange in Fort Garry Horse, arranged [illegible] of 4 horses & local treatment of Army 5th	
			The days not referred to [illegible] office [illegible] [illegible] [illegible] [illegible] [illegible]	
			V.J. [illegible] Maj AVC ADVS 5th Cav Div	

Instructions regarding War Diaries and Intelligence Summaries are contained in F. S. Regs., Part II. and the Staff Manual respectively. Title pages will be prepared in manuscript.

WAR DIARY
or
INTELLIGENCE SUMMARY.
(Erase heading not required.)

Army Form C. 2118.

Place	Date	Hour	Summary of Events and Information	Remarks and references to Appendices

Summary of Veterinary Wastage for Month of January 1917

Remaining	Admissions	Cured	Evacuated	Died	Destroyed	Remaining	Remarks
158	471	266	192	3	7	161	

Cause of death Pneumonia 1 Fracture Vertebrae 1 Strangulation of Intestine 1
Reasons for destruction Fracture 1 Pneumonia 1 Wounds 3 Injuries 2

Mange incidence by weeks 15 35 12 15 Total 77

[illegible]
2.2.17

[illegible] Maj ...
ADVS 1st Cav Div

Instructions regarding War Diaries and Intelligence Summaries are contained in F. S. Regs., Part II. and the Staff Manual respectively. Title pages will be prepared in manuscript.

Jan./17

WAR DIARY
or
INTELLIGENCE SUMMARY.
(*Erase heading not required.*)

Army Form C. 2118.

A.D.V.S. 5th Cavalry Division

Place	Date	Hour	Summary of Events and Information	Remarks and references to Appendices
	1.1.17		Made arrangements with G.O.C. Secunderabad & Canadian Cavalry Brigade for elementary veterinary demonstrations to junior officers & senior N.C.O.s of units	
	2.1.17		Arranged veterinary demonstrations for junior officers & senior N.C.O. with G.O.C. Ambala Cavalry Bde. Inspected R.H.A. Brigade Ammunition Column & X Battery R.H.A. discovered an outbreak of mange in X Battery	
	3.1.17		G.O.C. inspected horses of Divisional Headquarters, inspected Auxiliary Horse Transport & Reserve Park with Veterinary Officer i/c	
	4.1.17		General inspection of X Battery R.H.A. found 19 cases of mange & whole unit in contact with mange cases. Made arrangements for treating mange cases & had [illegible] lecture to Officers & N.C.Os R.H.A. on Mange	
	5.1.17		M.V.S. Ambala Brigade inspected. Confirm diagnosis of mange in X Battery. Completed arrangements for local treatment	
	7.1.17		Inspected M.V.S. Lucknow Cavalry Bde & saw traumatic cases	
	8.1.17		D.D.V.S. Cavalry Corps inspected conditions for treating mange in R.H.A.	
	9.1.17		Inspected mange treatment at X Battery conditions for treatment favourable	
	10.1.17		Inspected M.V.S. Canadian Cavalry Brigade & saw traumatic cases	

2353 Wt. W2544/1454 700,000 5/15 D. D. & L. A.D.S.S./Forms/C. 2118.

Army Form C. 2118.

WAR DIARY
or
INTELLIGENCE SUMMARY.

(Erase heading not required.)

Instructions regarding War Diaries and Intelligence Summaries are contained in F. S. Regs., Part II. and the Staff Manual respectively. Title pages will be prepared in manuscript.

Place	Date	Hour	Summary of Events and Information	Remarks and references to Appendices
	11.1.17		Inspection A Battery RHA. Progress of Mange. Horses improving	
	12.1.17		Inspection M.G.S. Ambala Brigade. Saw Mange outbreak of Machine Gun Squadron	
			Inspection Ambala Machine Gun Squadron	
	13.1.17		G.O.C. inspected Auxiliary Horse Transport Coy & Remount Park. Visited X Battery.	
			Lieutenant T.G.E. GALLIE [illegible] placed on sick list	
	14.1.17		Inspection M.G.S. Secunderabad. Saw [illegible] cases	
	15.1.17		Inspection M.G.S. Ambala Cavalry Bde. Saw Machine [illegible] from outbreak of Mange. Inspection	
			Field Squadron R.E. Evacuated 1 case Mange	
	18.1.17		Inspection RCHA evacuated several cases of Mange especially from B Battery. Arranged	
			treatment of civilian horses affected with Mange in area occupied by British troops	
	19.1.17		Inspection Auxiliary Horse Transport Coy & Remount Park. Also Canadian Mobile Vety Section	
	20.1.17		Inspection X Battery Mange cases. Lieutenant GALLIE rejoined from sick list	
	21.1.17		Inspection for Mange RCHA found 21 cases Mange but method of treatment [illegible] working	
			order. Arranged for supply of material & staff for dealing with Mange in Unit lines	
	22.1.17		Went to No 5 Veterinary Hospital Abbeville	
	23.1.17		DADVS Cavalry Corps. Cast horses for Remount reasons at [illegible] Canadian Cavalry Bde	

2353 Wt. W2544/1454 700,000 5/15 D. D. & L. A.D.S.S./Forms/C. 2118.

Instructions regarding War Diaries and Intelligence Summaries are contained in F. S. Regs., Part II. and the Staff Manual respectively. Title pages will be prepared in manuscript.

WAR DIARY
or
INTELLIGENCE SUMMARY.
(Erase heading not required.)

Army Form C. 2118.

Place	Date	Hour	Summary of Events and Information	Remarks and references to Appendices
	23.1.17		Lieutenant GALLIE AVC [illegible] unit. Applied for reinforcement	
	24.1.17		Inspected Canadian Machine Gun Squadron & [illegible]. Saw [illegible] case at M.V.S.	
	25.1.17		Saw Ambulance horse transferred by [illegible] stable & [illegible] for Mange.	
	26.1.17		Inspected Mange cases under treatment at RCHA & X Battery RCHA.	
	27.1.17		Inspected M.V.S. Ambulance & [illegible] unit of 9th Hussars ~~[illegible]~~ Lieutenant GALLIE [illegible] UK. Capt F.W. MEDLOCK AVC arrived & has appointed [illegible] of [illegible] in place of Lieut GALLIE AVC	
	29.1.17		Inspected M.V.S. Canadian Cavalry Bde & [illegible]	
	30.1.17		Inspected A Battery & Bde Hqrs RCHA arranged [illegible] of [illegible] Mange case at Fort Garry Horse	
	31.1.17		Inspected [illegible] case of Mange at Fort Garry Horse arranged [illegible] of 4 horses & local treatment of any other	
			[illegible]	

V.J. [illegible] Maj AVC
ADVS 1st Cav Div.

2353 Wt. W2544/1454 700,000 5/15 D. D. & L. A.D.S.S. Forms/C. 2118.

Instructions regarding War Diaries and Intelligence Summaries are contained in F. S. Regs., Part II. and the Staff Manual respectively. Title pages will be prepared in manuscript.

WAR DIARY
or
INTELLIGENCE SUMMARY.
(*Erase heading not required.*)

Army Form C. 2118.

Place	Date	Hour	Summary of Events and Information	Remarks and references to Appendices

Summary of Veterinary workload for Month of January 1917

Remaining	Admissions	Cured	Evacuated	Died	Destroyed	Remaining	Remarks
158	471	266	192	3	7	161.	

Causes of death Pneumonia 1 Fracture [illegible] 1 Strangulation of Intestine 1
Reasons for destruction Fracture 1 Pneumonia 1 Wounds 3 Injuries 2

Mange Incidence by weeks. 15. 35 12 15 Total 77.

D[illegible]
2.2.17.

S. J. [illegible] Maj [illegible]
A.D.V.S. 4th Cav Div

2353 Wt. W2544/1454 700,000 5/15 D. D. & L. A.D.S.S. Forms/C 2118.

Instructions regarding War Diaries and Intelligence Summaries are contained in F. S. Regs., Part II. and the Staff Manual respectively. Title pages will be prepared in manuscript.

WAR DIARY
or
INTELLIGENCE SUMMARY.
(Erase heading not required.)

Vol. VIII

Army Form C. 2118.

A.D.V.S. 5th Cavalry Division

Place	Date	Hour	Summary of Events and Information	Remarks and references to Appendices
Field	1.2.17		Inspected all sick animals of divisional troops with Veterinary Officer i/c, in particular Mange cases of RHA Brigade	
	2.2.17		Made enquiries into cases of deaths among horses of Auxiliary Horse Transport Coy. Suggestion of Malice not confirmed	
	3.2.17		Inspection of Lord Strathcona's Horse by Divisional Commander, inspected A. Mobile Vety Section. Evacuation to L.O.C. of horse casualties has stopped owing to congestion of base hospitals	
	4.2.17		Inspected M.V.S. [illegible] Bde arranged for local treatment of horse casualties	
	5.2.17		Heavy snow fall, inspected Canadian Mobile Veterinary Section, saw Regimental Veterinary Officers re Anti Mange measures	
	6.2.17		Inspection of X Battery RHA especially Mange cases. progress satisfactory, attended P.M. examination of case ~~at~~ of XX Deccan Horse which died without apparent cause,	
	7.2.17		Inspection of Canadian Machine Gun Squadron & Fort Garry Horse by G.O.C. [illegible] regiments horses were looking well	
	8.2.17		Inspected Ambala Mobile Vety Section & R.E. Labour parties working in FORÊT DEU. Inspected Auxiliary H.T. Coy & Reserve Park	
	9.2.17		Inspection of Royal Canadian Dragoons by Divisional Commander. Mange inspection of Fort Garry Horse	

Instructions regarding War Diaries and Intelligence Summaries are contained in F. S. Regs., Part II. and the Staff Manual respectively. Title pages will be prepared in manuscript.

WAR DIARY
or
INTELLIGENCE SUMMARY.
(Erase heading not required.)

Army Form C. 2118.

Place	Date	Hour	Summary of Events and Information	Remarks and references to Appendices
			segregated 8 cases of Mange – attended board of examination into the merits of a field forge, found it was quite useless –	
	10.2.17		Office routine	
	11.2.17		Inspected Secbad M G Section saw Brigade Vety Officer, OC M.V.S. A came to explain neglect of divisional orders.	
	12.2.17		Inspection of Field Squadron 7th Dragoon Guards + Secbad M.V.S. by Divisional Commander. Visited ADVS 4th Cavalry Division re use of Horse dip at [illegible]VILLE	
	13.2.17		Inspected M G Section Secbad also AMVS Canadian Brigade Inspected Regimental lines of RCHA, established Mange lines –	
	14.2.17		Inspection R.H.A. + RCHA by Divisional Commander	
	15.2.17		Inspection of all Regimental [illegible] Canadian Brigade (RCD. L.S.H. + F.G. Horse) saw Brigade re establishment of Mange lines	
	16.2.17		Saw Regimental [illegible] of Machine Gun Squadron + units of Secbad Brigade, Thaw set in after long period of frost.	
	17.2.17		Inspection of Cavalry Field Ambulance + Mobile Vety Section Canadian + Ambala Cavalry Bdes ~~[illegible]~~ Visited Ambala MVS saw treatment cases	

2353 Wt. W2544/1454 700,000 5/15 D. D. & L. A.D.S.S./Forms/C. 2118.

Army Form C. 2118.

Instructions regarding War Diaries and Intelligence Summaries are contained in F. S. Regs., Part II. and the Staff Manual respectively. Title pages will be prepared in manuscript.

WAR DIARY
or
INTELLIGENCE SUMMARY.
(Erase heading not required.)

Place	Date	Hour	Summary of Events and Information	Remarks and references to Appendices
	18.2.17		Inspection Signal Squadron & Auxilliary H.T. Coy latter unit in bad condition 55 horses struck off duty	
	19.2.17		Inspection Machine Gun Squadron Canadian Cavalry Bde Inspection M.V.S. A. & RCHA	
	20.2.17		Inspection VIII Hussars IX Horse XVII Lancers by Chief Commander Inspection of N Battery RHA. arranged evacuation as ataller case of 8 horses.	
	21.2.17		DDVS Cavalry Corps. Inspection Many stables RCHA Inspection of Field Squadron, gave Veterinary lecture Chief School	
	22.2.17		Office routine	
	23.2.17		Inspection M.V.S. Ambulance Cavalry Bde	
	24.2.17		Inspection of Deccan Horse, Poona Horse & 9th Hodsons Horse by Chief Commander. Visited D.V.S at Hdqrs L.o.C	
	25.2.17		Met ADVS 4th Cavalry Div & O.C. Field Squadron at Horse Dip at FRIVILLE re finishing off the tank & getting it into working order. Evacuation of L.o.C re. Stand for horse evacuation.	
	26.2.17		Inspection M.V.S. A. Canadian Brigade also Regimental units of M.G. Squadron & RCHA	
	27.2.17		Inspection A.H.T. Transport Coy. Considerable improvement as a result of change of C.O. Practised the method of dipping horses at FRIVILLE by means of M.V. Sections	

2353 Wt. W2544/1454 700,000 5/15 D. D. & L. A.D.S.S. Forms/C. 2118.

Instructions regarding War Diaries and Intelligence Summaries are contained in F. S. Regs., Part II. and the Staff Manual respectively. Title pages will be prepared in manuscript.

Army Form C. 2118.

WAR DIARY
or
INTELLIGENCE SUMMARY.

(Erase heading not required.)

Place	Date	Hour	Summary of Events and Information	Remarks and references to Appendices
	28.2.17		Office routine	
			Sick horses for Month of February 1917.	

Remaining	Admitted	Cured	Evacuated	Died	Destroyed	Remaining
161	460	237	54	14	28	288

Mange incidence by units 31. 12. 64 6. = 113

N.B. the high incidence in [illegible] the 3rd unit is represented by the inclusion of a large number of surplus animals & in contacts to the RCHA

Mortality. Deaths were due to Exhaustion 3 Colic 8 Chronic disease 3
Destructions were due to debility & age 12 Wounds 7 Fracture 6 Lameness & Chronic disease 2

[illegible] Maj AVC
ADVS 5th Cav Div

2353 Wt. W2544/1454 700,000 5/15 D. D. & L. A.D.S.S. Forms/C 2118.

Instructions regarding War Diaries and Intelligence Summaries are contained in F. S. Regs., Part II. and the Staff Manual respectively. Title pages will be prepared in manuscript.

Feb/17

WAR DIARY
or
INTELLIGENCE SUMMARY.
(Erase heading not required.)

Army Form C. 2118.

A.D.V.S. 5th Cavalry Division

Place	Date	Hour	Summary of Events and Information	Remarks and references to Appendices
Field	1.2.17		Inspected all sick animals of divisional [illegible] with Veterinary Officer [illegible], in particular [illegible] cases of RHA Brigade	
	2.2.17		Made enquiries into cases of deaths among horses of Auxiliary Horse Transport Coy. Suggestion of [illegible] not enforced	
	3.2.17		Inspection of Lord Strathcona's Horse by Divisional Commander. Inspected A Mobile Vety Section. [illegible] to G.O.C. of horse casualties [illegible]	
	4.2.17		Inspected M.V.S. Lucknow Bde arranged for local treatment of horse casualties.	
	5.2.17		Heavy snow fall. Inspected Canadian Mobile Veterinary Section [illegible] Regimental Veterinary Officer re [illegible]	
	6.2.17		Inspection of X Battery RHA [illegible] [illegible] P.M. [illegible] of [illegible] horse [illegible] without [illegible] cause	
	7.2.17		Inspection of Canadian Machine Gun Squadron & Fort Garry Horse by G.O.C. [illegible] horses [illegible] well	
	8.2.17		Inspected Ambala Mobile Vety Section & RE [illegible] FORET D'EU	
			Inspected Auxiliary H T Coy & Remount Park	
	9.2.17		Inspection of Royal Canadian Dragoons by Divisional Commander. [illegible] of Fort Garry Horse	

2353 Wt. W2544/1454 700,000 5/15 D. D. & L. A.D.S.S. Forms/C 2118.

Army Form C. 2118.

WAR DIARY
or
INTELLIGENCE SUMMARY.
(Erase heading not required.)

Instructions regarding War Diaries and Intelligence Summaries are contained in F. S. Regs., Part II. and the Staff Manual respectively. Title pages will be prepared in manuscript.

Place	Date	Hour	Summary of Events and Information	Remarks and references to Appendices
			segregation & cases of mange – attended board of examination into the merits of a field forge; found it was quite useless —	
	10.2.17		Office routine	
	11.2.17		Inspection Lucknow M.V. Section saw Brigade Vety Officer OC M.V.S. re case to [illegible] in light of divisional orders.	
	12.2.17		Inspection of Field Squadron 7th Dragoon Guards & Lucknow M.V.S. by Divisional Commander. Visited ADVS 4th Cavalry Division re use of horse dip at TRIVILLE	
	13.2.17		Inspection M.V. Section Lucknow also A.M.V.S. Canadian Brigade. Inspection Regimental lines of RCHA established [illegible] mange lines	
	14.2.17		Inspection R.H.A. & RCHA by Divisional Commander	
	15.2.17		Inspection of all Regimental units Canadian Brigade (RCD, L.S.H. & F.G. Horse) saw Brigade re establishment of mange lines	
	16.2.17		Saw Regimental units of Machine Gun Squadron & units of Lucknow Brigade. Horses not [illegible] after long period of frost.	
	17.2.17		Inspection of Cavalry Field Ambulance & Mobile Vety Section Canadian & Ambala Cavalry Brigades. ~~saw~~ Visited Ambala M.V.S. saw treatment cases	

2353 Wt. W2544/1454 700,000 5/15 D. D. & L. A.D.S.S. Forms/C 2118.

Army Form C. 2118.

WAR DIARY
or
INTELLIGENCE SUMMARY.
(Erase heading not required.)

Instructions regarding War Diaries and Intelligence Summaries are contained in F. S. Regs., Part II. and the Staff Manual respectively. Title pages will be prepared in manuscript.

Place	Date	Hour	Summary of Events and Information	Remarks and references to Appendices
	18.2.17		Inspection Signal Squadron & Auxiliary H.T. Coy. Cattle [illegible] in fair condition. 55 horses struck off duty	
	19.2.17		Inspection Machine Gun Squadron Canadian Cavalry Bde. Inspection M.G.S.A. & R.C.H.A.	
	20.2.17		Inspection VIII Hussars, IX Horse, XVIII Lancers by Divl Commander. Inspection of N Battery R.H.A. arranged evacuation and isolation case of [illegible] horses.	
	21.2.17		O.D.V.S. Cavalry Corps inspected Many stables R.C.H.A. Inspection of Field Squadron. Gave veterinary lecture Divl School	
	22.2.17		Office routine	
	23.2.17		Inspection M.V.S. Ambala Cavalry Bde	
	24.2.17		Inspection of Deccan Horse, Poona Horse & 9th Hodson Horse by Divl Commander. Visited D.V.S. at H.Qrs L.o.C.	
	25.2.17		Met A.D.V.S. 4th Cavalry Divn & O.C. Field Squadron at Horse Dept at FRÉVILLE re furnishing of the [illegible] & [illegible] evacuation of L.o.C. [illegible] for horse casualties.	
	26.2.17		Inspection M.G.S.A. Canadian Brigade also Regimental units of M.G. Squadron & R.C.H.A.	
	27.2.17		Inspection A.H.T. Transport Coy. Considerable improvement as a result of change of C.O. Practising the methods of clipping horses at FRÉVILLE by means of M/c machines.	

2353 Wt. W2544/1454 700,000 5/15 D. D. & L. A.D.S.S. Forms/C. 2118.

Army Form C. 2118.

Instructions regarding War Diaries and Intelligence Summaries are contained in F. S. Regs., Part II. and the Staff Manual respectively. Title pages will be prepared in manuscript.

WAR DIARY
or
INTELLIGENCE SUMMARY.

(Erase heading not required.)

Place	Date	Hour	Summary of Events and Information	Remarks and references to Appendices
	28 2 17		Office routine	
			Sick horses for month of February 1917.	

Remaining	Admitted	Cured	Evacuated	Died	Destroyed	Remaining
161	460	237	54	14	28	288

Mange cases evacuated by trucks 31. 12 64 6 = 113

N.B. The high admissions in ~~[illegible]~~ the 3rd week is explained by the inclusion of a large number of [illegible] & [illegible] contacts in the RCHA

Mortality. Deaths were due to Exhaustion 3 Colic 8 [illegible] disease 3

Destructions were due to debility & age 12 wounds 7 Fractures 1 lameness 4 [illegible] diseases 2

[illegible signature] Major [illegible]
ADVS 5th Can Div

2353 Wt. W2544/1454 700,000 5/15 D. D. & L. A.D.S.S. Forms/C. 2118.

Instructions regarding War Diaries and Intelligence Summaries are contained in F. S. Regs., Part II. and the Staff Manual respectively. Title Pages will be prepared in manuscript.

WAR DIARY
or
INTELLIGENCE SUMMARY
(Erase heading not required.)

Vol IX

Army Form C. 2118.

A.D.V.S. 1st Cavalry Division

March 1917

Place	Date	Hour	Summary of Events and Information	Remarks and references to Appendices
	1.3		Inspection horses in Regtl units [illegible] of [illegible] to [illegible] Horse [illegible] & Battery	
	2.3		Divisional scheme for Administrative [illegible] by [illegible] G S	
	3.3		Inspection M.V. Section Ambala Brigade [illegible] horses undergoing treatment	
	4.3		Inspection M.V. Section [illegible] Brigade & Regimental units of 7 D.G.	
	5.3		Inspection M.V. Section Canadian Brigade & [illegible] demonstration at [illegible] at M.V.E.?	
	6.3		Saw Regimental units & two squadrons of R.C. Dragoons & Regimental units of Auxiliary H.T. Company	
	7.3		O. A.D.V.S. Cavalry Corps [illegible] for [illegible] at [illegible]	
	[illegible].3		Inspection Regtl units Ambala Cavalry Brigade [illegible] Brigade [illegible] M.V.S. [illegible] Auxiliary H.T. Coy & others	

2449 Wt. W14957/M90 750,000 1/16 J.B.C. & A. Forms/C.2118/12.

Army Form C. 2118.

Instructions regarding War Diaries and Intelligence Summaries are contained in F. S. Regs., Part II. and the Staff Manual respectively. Title Pages will be prepared in manuscript.

WAR DIARY
or
INTELLIGENCE SUMMARY

(Erase heading not required.)

Place	Date	Hour	Summary of Events and Information	Remarks and references to Appendices
	11.3.		Inspection Canadian M.G.S. & [illegible] M.G.S. [illegible] Regimental [illegible] of [illegible] & Machine Gun Squadron.	
	12.3		Division [illegible] placed on 48 hours [illegible] Captain F.W. MEDLOCK [illegible]	
	13.3		Inspection Mange [illegible] R.C.H.A. Conference of [illegible] Officers. Canadian Cavalry Bde	
	14.3		Attending Conference at Q Office [illegible] preliminary arrangements [illegible] the [illegible] of [illegible]	
	15.3		Inspection of A.H. Transport [illegible] D.D.S.&T. Corps, Captain Veterinary Conference on [illegible] of M.G. Section during [illegible]	
	16.3		Captain J.W. MORAN [illegible] for duty, [illegible] Captain F.W. MEDLOCK [illegible] unit	
	17.3		Inspection of Remount transfer from 4th Cavalry division an extraordinarily bad lot. [illegible] Auxiliary H.T. Coy in afternoon.	

2449 Wt. W14957/M90 750,000 1/16 J.B.C. & A. Forms/C.2118/12.

Instructions regarding War Diaries and Intelligence Summaries are contained in F. S. Regs., Part II. and the Staff Manual respectively. Title Pages will be prepared in manuscript.

WAR DIARY
or
INTELLIGENCE SUMMARY

(Erase heading not required.)

Army Form C. 2118.

Place	Date	Hour	Summary of Events and Information	Remarks and references to Appendices
	[illegible] 2		Inspection [illegible] Divisional Troops with Capt. MORAN [illegible]	
	[illegible] 3		Received orders to move Eastwards. Canadian Cavalry Brigade [illegible]	
	20.3		Remainder of Division marched from [illegible] area to PERONNE area completing the	
	21		distance in four marches by SERARPONT PONT de METZ . CERISY	
	22		PERONNE. Severe weather [illegible] conditions, high winds, frost [illegible] being	
	23		constantly in evidence. 29 horses belonging to units of the division were left behind on the line of March being billeted with farmers & local inhabitants	
	24		On these dates [illegible] & Canadian Cavalry Brigades were in action. Secunderabad Brigade being	
	25		in reserve. Mobile Veterinary Sections of the two former Brigades were attached to the Brigade	
	26		[illegible] & Secunderabad M.V.S. [illegible] & attached to [illegible] Divisional Troops	
	27		the two former [illegible] receiving [illegible] from the Brigades the latter [illegible] for the division	

2449 Wt. W14957/M90 750,000 1/16 J.B.C. & A. Forms/C.2118/12.

Instructions regarding War Diaries and Intelligence Summaries are contained in F. S. Regs., Part II. and the Staff Manual respectively. Title Pages will be prepared in manuscript.

WAR DIARY
or
INTELLIGENCE SUMMARY
(Erase heading not required.)

Army Form C. 2118.

Place	Date	Hour	Summary of Events and Information	Remarks and references to Appendices
			During the operation 162 horses were hit by bullets or shell fire 42 were killed & 6 destroyed on account of wounds. 80 horses were evacuated to L. of C. of which the greater number were actual battle casualties	
	25.3		Inspection Canadian M.V.S. & M.V.S. with B echelon arranged evacuation of 80 horses with R.T.O.	
	29.3		Brigades moved westwards. Our Artillery Brigades in the action [illegible] horses [illegible] [illegible].	
	30.3		Divisional Headquarters moved to [illegible] ABBATOIR [illegible]. Remounts arrived for Division [illegible] from ROUEN [illegible] detrained at CERISY.	
	31.3		Inspection Artillery M.V. Section [illegible] Brigade [illegible] [illegible] Artillery [illegible] Brigade [illegible] M.V.S. [illegible] Brigade [illegible], [illegible] all [illegible] to Base.	
			[illegible] Maj [illegible] A.D.V.S. 5th Cav Div	

2449 Wt. W14957/M90 750,000 1/16 J.B.C. & A. Forms/C.2118/12.

Instructions regarding War Diaries and Intelligence Summaries are contained in F. S. Regs., Part II. and the Staff Manual respectively. Title Pages will be prepared in manuscript.

WAR DIARY
or
INTELLIGENCE SUMMARY
(Erase heading not required.)

Vol 10

Army Form. C. 2118.

ADVS 1st Cavalry Division

Place	Date	Hour	Summary of Events and Information	Remarks and references to Appendices
April 1917	1.		Office routine	
	2.		Inspection Auxiliary H.T. Coy & Reserve Park for the [illegible] of evacuating horses on account of Debility.	
	4th		Inspection M.V.S [illegible] Cavalry Bde re evacuation of horses from X Battery R.H.A. on account of debility. Captain EARLY Ave reported for duty i/c Canadian Cavalry Bde	
	5th		Inspection M.V.S Canadian Cavalry Bde saw all evacuation cases:-	
	6th		Inspection 5 Cav Div, [illegible] squadron, also evacuation from Section Brigade & Regimental [illegible] of that Brigade	
	10th		DDVS [illegible] [illegible] [illegible] horses of N Battery. RHA reported as unable to move on account of debilitated state of their animals	
	11th		Saw special sick cases 7 DG & N Battery	

2449 Wt. W14957/M90 750,000 1/16 J.B.C. & A. Forms/C.2118/12.

Instructions regarding War Diaries and Intelligence Summaries are contained in F. S. Regs., Part II. and the Staff Manual respectively. Title Pages will be prepared in manuscript.

WAR DIARY
or
INTELLIGENCE SUMMARY
(Erase heading not required.)

Army Form C. 2118.

Place	Date	Hour	Summary of Events and Information	Remarks and references to Appendices
	12th		Enquiry as to case of STOMATITIS in 7th D Guards. Arranged for dealing with contagious diseases in Brigades by exchange with M G [illegible].	
	13th		DDVS arranged transfer of horses from 258 Battery to [illegible] Battery, but by order of Divl Commander exchange was stopped. Inspection of sick horses R.C.D. with Vety Officer.	
	14th		Division marched to area bordering OMIGNON river ~~[illegible]~~ over Secunderabad Brigade in line of March.	
	15th		344 remounts arrived & were distributed to units	
	16th		Inspection Ammunition Column & Reserve Park – Captain J. HUGHES AVC placed on sick list	
	19th		Inspection Secunderabad M.G.S & regimental units, Secunderabad Brigade :–	

Instructions regarding War Diaries and Intelligence Summaries are contained in F. S. Regs., Part II. and the Staff Manual respectively. Title Pages will be prepared in manuscript.

WAR DIARY
or
INTELLIGENCE SUMMARY
(Erase heading not required.)

Army Form C. 2118.

Place	Date	Hour	Summary of Events and Information	Remarks and references to Appendices
	20.		Inspection Lord Strathcona's Horse, high proportion of thin horses. Inspection regimental units R.C. Dragoons:–	
	21		Inspection Regimental units Seeley's Brigade – Captain Stephens [illegible] to Strathconas	
	22		Inspection R.C. Dragoons, Canadian M.G. Squadron & C.F.A. all looking much better:–	
	23		Inspection A.M.V.S. Canadian Brigade. R.C.H.A. horses coming on well – many long horses:–	
	24		Discussed value of I.C.B. horses for various services with O.C. [illegible] Stores, Remounts & Brigade Commanders:–	
	25		G.O.C. inspected R.C.H.A. & R.C. Dragoons. Discussed I.C.B. horses with C.O.s	

2449 Wt. W14957/M90 750,000 1/16 J.B.C. & A. Forms/C.2118/12.

Army Form C. 2118.

WAR DIARY
or
INTELLIGENCE SUMMARY

(Erase heading not required.)

Instructions regarding War Diaries and Intelligence Summaries are contained in F. S. Regs., Part II. and the Staff Manual respectively. Title Pages will be prepared in manuscript.

Place	Date	Hour	Summary of Events and Information	Remarks and references to Appendices
			of units in Ambala Brigade - inspection M.V.S Ambala Brigade	
	27		Inspection M.V.S. 1st Canadian Brigade also night route Canadian Brigade	
	29		Inspection Ancillary, H.T. Coy & Ammunition Column	
	30		Inspection Regimental units Ambala Brigade	
			Working during month of April 1917	

Remaining 1.4.17	admissions	cured	evacuated	died	destroyed	Remaining May 1st
189	939	549	282	40	44	213

Army Form C. 2118.

Instructions regarding War Diaries and Intelligence Summaries are contained in F. S. Regs., Part II. and the Staff Manual respectively. Title Pages will be prepared in manuscript.

WAR DIARY
or
INTELLIGENCE SUMMARY

(Erase heading not required.)

Place	Date	Hour	Summary of Events and Information	Remarks and references to Appendices
			Deaths resulted as follows. Heart disease 3 exhaustion 20 Gunshot wounds 3 Colic 6 Diseases 8 = 40 Destructions were necessitated for the following reasons. Exhaustion 29 wounds 7 fractures 7 disease 1 = 44. Contagious disease occurred in the division as follows. Mange 26 Cellulitis 7 D Hayes [illegible] 5th Cav Div [illegible] Major [illegible] A.D.V.S. 5th Cav Div	

2449 Wt. W14957/M90 750,000 1/16 J.B.C. & A. Forms/C.2118/12.

Instructions regarding War Diaries and Intelligence Summaries are contained in F. S. Regs., Part II. and the Staff Manual respectively. Title Pages will be prepared in manuscript.

WAR DIARY
or
INTELLIGENCE SUMMARY
(Erase heading not required.)

Army Form C. 2118.

ADVS 5th Cavalry Division

Place	Date	Hour	Summary of Events and Information	Remarks and references to Appendices
April 1917	1.		Office routine	
	2.		Inspection Ambulance H.T. Coy & Reserve Park for the purpose of evacuating horses on account of Debility	
	4th		Inspection M.V.S Ambala Cavalry Bde re evacuation of horses from X Battery R.H.A on account of debility. Captain EARLY A.V.C reported for duty in Canadian Cavalry Bde.	
	5th		Inspection M.V.S Canadian Cavalry Bde saw all evacuation cases.	
	6th		Inspection 5 Cav Div Signal Squadron also evacuation from Lucknow Brigade & Regimental sick of that Brigade.	
	10th		DDVS Fourth Army inspected horses of N Battery R.H.A reported as unfit to move on account of debilitated state of their animals	
	11th		Saw special sick case 7 D.G. & N Battery	

2449 Wt. W14957/M90 750,000 1/16 J.B.C. & A. Forms/C.2118/12.

Instructions regarding War Diaries and Intelligence Summaries are contained in F. S. Regs., Part II. and the Staff Manual respectively. Title Pages will be prepared in manuscript.

WAR DIARY
or
INTELLIGENCE SUMMARY

(Erase heading not required.)

Army Form C. 2118.

Place	Date	Hour	Summary of Events and Information	Remarks and references to Appendices
	12th		Enquiry into case of STOMATITIS in 7th D. Guards. Arranges for dealing with all cases in divisions in Brigades ~~[illegible]~~ by exchange with M.V. Sections	
	13th		DDVS arranges transfer of horses from 258 Battery to [illegible] Battery by order of Divl Commander exchange [illegible] - inspection of sick horses R.C.D with [illegible] officer	
	14th		Division marches to area bordering [illegible] ~~[illegible]~~ over Section Brigade on line of March	
	15th		344 remounts arrive & were distributed to units	
	16th		Inspection Ammunition Column & Remount Park - [illegible] J. HUGHES AVC placed on sick list	
	19th		Inspection Section M.V.S. & regimental [illegible] Section Brigade area	

Army Form C. 2118.

Instructions regarding War Diaries and Intelligence Summaries are contained in F. S. Regs., Part II. and the Staff Manual respectively. Title Pages will be prepared in manuscript.

WAR DIARY
or
INTELLIGENCE SUMMARY
(Erase heading not required.)

Place	Date	Hour	Summary of Events and Information	Remarks and references to Appendices
	20.		Inspection Lord Strathcona's Horse high proportion of thin horses – inspection [illegible] with R.C. Dragoons	
	21		Inspection Regimental [illegible] Secunderabad Brigade – Captain [illegible] [illegible] to [illegible]	
	22		Inspection R.C. Dragoons Canadian M.G. Squadron & C.F.A. all looking much better.	
	23		Inspection A. M.G.1 Canadian Brigade. R.C.H.A. horses coming on well – many young horses	
	24		Discussed value of I.C.B. horses for [illegible] [illegible] with O.C. [illegible] [illegible] [illegible] & Brigade Commander	
	25		G.O.C. inspected R.C.H.A. & R.C. Dragoons. Discussed I.C.B. horses with C.O.	

2449 Wt. W14957/M90 750,000 1/16 J.B.C. & A. Forms/C.2118/12.

Instructions regarding War Diaries and Intelligence Summaries are contained in F. S. Regs., Part II. and the Staff Manual respectively. Title Pages will be prepared in manuscript.

WAR DIARY
or
INTELLIGENCE SUMMARY
(Erase heading not required.)

Army Form C. 2118.

Place	Date	Hour	Summary of Events and Information	Remarks and references to Appendices
			[illegible] in Artillery Brigade - Inspection M.V.S Artillery Brigade	
	27		Inspection M.V.S, R Canadian Brigade also night ride Canadian Brigade	
	29		Inspection Ancillary, HQ Coy & Ammunition Column	
	30		Inspection Regimental [illegible] Artillery Brigade	
			Working during month of April 1917	

Remaining 1.4.17	admissions	Cured	evacuations	died	discharged	Remaining, [illegible]
189	939	549	282	40	44	213

Army Form C. 2118.

WAR DIARY
or
INTELLIGENCE SUMMARY
(Erase heading not required.)

Instructions regarding War Diaries and Intelligence Summaries are contained in F. S. Regs., Part II. and the Staff Manual respectively. Title Pages will be prepared in manuscript.

Place	Date	Hour	Summary of Events and Information	Remarks and references to Appendices
			Deaths occurred as follows. Heart disease 3 exhaustion 20 Gunshot wound 3 Colic 6 Disease 8 = 40	
			Destructions were necessitated for the following reasons. Exhaustion 29 wounds 7 fractures 7 disease 1 = 44.	
			Contagious disease occurred in the division as follows. Mange 25 Cellulitis 7.	
			[illegible] 5th Cav Div	
			Holmes Maj ADVS 5th Cav Div	

2449 Wt. W14957/M90 750,000 1/16 J.B.C. & A. Forms/C.2118/12.

Instructions regarding War Diaries and Intelligence Summaries are contained in F. S. Regs., Part II. and the Staff Manual respectively. Title Pages will be prepared in manuscript.

WAR DIARY
or
INTELLIGENCE SUMMARY
(Erase heading not required.)

Army Form C. 2118.

VOL XI

ADVS 5th Cavalry Division May 1917.

Place	Date	Hour	Summary of Events and Information	Remarks and references to Appendices
May	1st		Inspection of horses first Squadron R.C.E. & Regimental sick Canadian Cavalry Brigade	
	2nd		Inspection of horses Divl Headquarters and X Battery R.H.A. Inspection of Brigade Transport A & B echelon, Ambala Brigade, by G.O.C. Division :-	
	3rd		Conference of A.D.V.S. at Office of D.D.V.S. Fourth Army, Divl Commander inspected A & B echelon Secunderabad Brigade - Inspection of horses, Reserve Park :-	
	4th		Inspection of horses N Battery, R.H.A for mange, found 9 cases - Arranged for dealing with a limited number of cases of mange in the division by converting Secunderabad M.V.S into a field mange hospital :-	
	6th		Inspection of mange station (Secunderabad) arrangements in good order & progress satisfactory	
	8th		Inspection Right line of divl horse units, also A. Canadian M.V.S. -	
	9th		Inspection of limber horses & Auxiliary H.T. Company	
	10th		Inspection of Sec-Bad M.V.S, Regimental lines R.C.D & C Squadron R.C. Dragoons	

2449 Wt. W14957/M90 750,000 1/16 J.B.C. & A. Forms/C.2118/12.

Instructions regarding War Diaries and Intelligence Summaries are contained in F. S. Regs., Part II. and the Staff Manual respectively. Title Pages will be prepared in manuscript.

WAR DIARY
or
INTELLIGENCE SUMMARY

(Erase heading not required.)

Army Form C. 2118.

Place	Date	Hour	Summary of Events and Information	Remarks and references to Appendices
May	12th		Inspection A. Canadian M.G. Section & Mange case Sect. M.V. Section :-	
	13th		Horse rugs were withdrawn from units & returned to Ordnance as follows. from Ambala Bde 11.5.17 from Secunderabad Bde & Divl Troops 12.5.17 from Canadian Bde 13.5.17	
	15th		Divl Headquarters moved to [illegible]BRESCOURT FARM – Inspected M.V.S. Ambala Cavalry Bde	
	17th		Inspected Ammunition Column & ~~Divl Ammunition Column~~ Auxiliary H.T. Coy re suspected Mange case:–	
	21st		Conference of all Veterinary Officers of the division to arrange a redistribution of duties with regard to the billets of Officers & position of units :–	
	22nd		Visited advanced Hdqrs Canadian Brigade & saw Regtl sick Ambala Bde :–	
	23rd		Inspection A. Canadian M.G. Section & Regimental sick Fort Garry Horse, also horses of L.S.H. & R.C. Dragoons.	
	24th		Saw Regtl sick Secunderabad Brigade, also 7th Dragoon Guards – inspected M.V.S. Secunderabad	
	25th		Inspection Auxiliary H.T. Company, Ammunition Column, Remount Park & Ambulance train	

2449 Wt. W14957/M90 750,000 1/16 J.B.C. & A. Forms/C.2118/12.

Instructions regarding War Diaries and Intelligence Summaries are contained in F. S. Regs., Part II. and the Staff Manual respectively. Title Pages will be prepared in manuscript.

WAR DIARY
or
INTELLIGENCE SUMMARY

(Erase heading not required.)

Army Form C. 2118.

Place	Date	Hour	Summary of Events and Information	Remarks and references to Appendices
May	26th		G.O.C. inspected hospital of divisional Veterinary - inspection MVS Section & Ambulance. Captain H.W. CRAIG (C) A.V.C. reported his arrival & was posted to Fort Garry Horse	
	27th		137 horses & 15 mules arrived at Railhead from Remount depot Boves for distribution to the division:-	
	28th		proceeded on leave of absence to the United Kingdom.	
			The days not specially noted routine duty was carried out -	
			Working summary for the month of May	

Remaining	admitted	Cured	Evacuated	died	destroyed	Remaining
213	506	433	69	12	12	193

During the month of ~~April~~ May the weekly incidence of Mange was as follows 13. 20. 16. 4 Total 53. the weekly incidence of Cellulitis was 3. 13. 2. 6, total 24.

2449 Wt. W14957/M90 750,000 1/16 J.B.C. & A. Forms/C.2118/12.

Army Form C. 2118.

WAR DIARY
or
INTELLIGENCE SUMMARY

(Erase heading not required.)

Instructions regarding War Diaries and Intelligence Summaries are contained in F. S. Regs., Part II. and the Staff Manual respectively. Title Pages will be prepared in manuscript.

Place	Date	Hour	Summary of Events and Information	Remarks and references to Appendices
			The causes of death in horses was as follows General diseases 4 Intestinal diseases 8 - - - [illegible] - - - - - Paralysis 3. Wounds 3 Fractures 5 Tetanus 1. W J Holmes(?) Maj AVC(?) ADVS 1st Ca Div	

2449 Wt. W14957/M90 750,000 1/16 J.B.C. & A. Forms/C.2118/12.

Army Form C. 2118.

Instructions regarding War Diaries and Intelligence Summaries are contained in F. S. Regs., Part II. and the Staff Manual respectively. Title Pages will be prepared in manuscript.

WAR DIARY
or
INTELLIGENCE SUMMARY
(Erase heading not required.)

ADVS 5th Cavalry Division May 1917

Place	Date	Hour	Summary of Events and Information	Remarks and references to Appendices
May	1st		Inspection of horses Field Squadron RE & Regimental [illegible] Canadian Cavalry Brigade	
	2nd		Inspection of horses Divl Headquarters and X Battery RHA. Inspection of Brigade Transport 4th & 5th Battalion Ambulance Brigade by G.O.C. Division	
	3rd		Conference of ADVS at office of DDVS Fourth Army. Divl Commander inspected 4th Battalion Secunderabad Brigade – Inspection of horses Rosenes Park	
	4th		Inspection of horses N Battery RHA for mange found 9 cases. Arrangements for dealing with a limited number of cases of mange in the division by converting Secunderabad M.V.S. into a field mange hospital	
	6th		Inspection of Mange Station (Secunderabad) arrangements in good order & progress satisfactory	
	8th		Inspected Right Section of Divl [illegible] with also A Canadian M.V.S.	
	9th		Inspection of [illegible] horses & Ambulance [illegible] Canadian Cavalry	
	10th		Inspection of Sialkot M.V.S. Regimental Section RCD & Canadian RC Dragoons	

2449 Wt. W14957/M90 750,000 1/16 J.B.C. & A. Forms/C.2118/12.

Army Form C. 2118.

WAR DIARY
or
INTELLIGENCE SUMMARY
(Erase heading not required.)

Instructions regarding War Diaries and Intelligence Summaries are contained in F. S. Regs., Part II. and the Staff Manual respectively. Title Pages will be prepared in manuscript.

Place	Date	Hour	Summary of Events and Information	Remarks and references to Appendices
May	12th		Inspection A. Canadian M G Section & Change over Secbad M G Section	
	13th		horse [illegible] [illegible] [illegible] for [illegible] [illegible] to advance [illegible] following. from Ambala Bde 4 S 17 from Secbad Bde & Div Troops 12 S 17 from Canadian Bde 13 S 17	
	15th		Div Headquarters moved to ABBESCOURT FARM – Inspection M G S Ambala Cavalry Bde	
	17th		Inspection Ammunition Column & Div Ammunition Column [illegible] [illegible] Many cars	
	20th		Conference of all [illegible] Officers of the division [illegible] [illegible] [illegible] [illegible] [illegible] [illegible] of [illegible]	
	22nd		Visited advanced Hdqrs Canadian Brigade saw Regt [illegible] Ambala Bde	
	23rd		Inspection A. Canadian M G Section & Regimental [illegible] Fort Garry Horse also lines of L S H & R C Dragoons.	
	24th		Saw Regt [illegible] Secbad Brigade also 7th Dragoon Guards – [illegible] M G S Secbad	
	25th		Inspection Auxiliary [illegible] Ammunition Column [illegible] [illegible] [illegible]	

Instructions regarding War Diaries and Intelligence Summaries are contained in F. S. Regs., Part II. and the Staff Manual respectively. Title Pages will be prepared in manuscript.

WAR DIARY
or
INTELLIGENCE SUMMARY
(Erase heading not required.)

Army Form C. 2118.

Place	Date	Hour	Summary of Events and Information	Remarks and references to Appendices
May	26th		G.O.C. inspected horses of Divisional [illegible] – inspection M.V.S. Section & Battalion	
			Captain H.W. CRAIG (C) A.V.C. [illegible] arrived from [illegible] to [illegible]	
	27th		137 horses & 15 mules arrived at [illegible] from Remount Depot [illegible] for distribution to the Division	
	28th		proceeded on leave of absence to the United Kingdom	
			The charge but especially [illegible] duty was [illegible]	
			Veterinary summary for the month of May.	
			Remaining 213; admitted 576; cured 433; evacuated 69; died 12; destroyed 12; Remaining 143	
			During the month of May the weekly incidence of Mange was as follows. 13. 20. 16. 4 Total 53. The weekly incidence of Cellulitis was 3. 13. 2. 6	Total 24

2449 Wt. W14957/M90 750,000 1/16 J.B.C. & A. Forms/C.2118/12.

Instructions regarding War Diaries and Intelligence Summaries are contained in F. S. Regs., Part II. and the Staff Manual respectively. Title Pages will be prepared in manuscript.

WAR DIARY
or
INTELLIGENCE SUMMARY
(Erase heading not required.)

Army Form C. 2118.

Place	Date	Hour	Summary of Events and Information	Remarks and references to Appendices
			The cause of death in horses was as follows. General diseases 4 [illegible] diseases 8	
			- - - destruction - - - - - Paralysis 3. Wounds 3 Fractures 5	
			Tetanus 1	
			[illegible] Maj [illegible]	
			ADVS 1st Ca Div	

2449 Wt. W14957/M90 750,000 1/16 J.B.C. & A. Forms/C.2118/12.

Instructions regarding War Diaries and Intelligence Summaries are contained in F. S. Regs., Part II. and the Staff Manual respectively. Title Pages will be prepared in manuscript.

WAR DIARY
or
INTELLIGENCE SUMMARY
(Erase heading not required.)

Army Form C. 2118.

ADVS 5th Cavalry Division

Place	Date	Hour	Summary of Events and Information	Remarks and references to Appendices
June	1917 1st to 12th		Absent in United Kingdom on ordinary leave.	
	13th		Inspection A Canadian Mobile Section. Ammunition Column & Reserve Park	
	14th		Inspection Divisional H.Qrs., Captain O GOGARTY under orders for duty with Cavalry Corps headquarters.	
	15th		Inspection Fort Garry Horse & Lord Strathcona's Horse - all much improved in condition	
	16th		Inspection Secunderabad Cavalry Bde by Divisional Commander	
	19th		Inspection A & B Batteries R.C.H.A. wagon lines also Canadian Field Ambulance	
	20th		Inspection Ambala Cavalry Bde by Divisional Commander - Inspection M.V.S. Ambala Cavalry Bde	
	21st		Remounts arrived at Railhead & D.D.R. cast unsuitable horses.	

2449 Wt. W14957/M90 750,000 1/16 J.B.C. & A. Forms/C.2118/12.

Army Form C. 2118.

Instructions regarding War Diaries and Intelligence Summaries are contained in F. S. Regs., Part II. and the Staff Manual respectively. Title Pages will be prepared in manuscript.

WAR DIARY
or
INTELLIGENCE SUMMARY

(Erase heading not required.)

Place	Date	Hour	Summary of Events and Information	Remarks and references to Appendices
June	22		Placed on sick in quarters list on account of boils	
	26th		Made arrangements for applying mallein test to horses of Ammunition Column ([illegible]) owing to detection of case of Glanders from this unit at the base —	
	29th		Inspection of horses of Div[l] Headquarters Reserve Park & Auxiliary H.T. Coy by Div[l] Commander	
	30th		taken off sick in quarters list	
			From 22.6.17 to 30.6.17 only office work & occasional duties could be performed by me & I was unable to appoint a substitute [illegible] on A.D.V.S.	
			A Monthly Wastage Summary is given overleaf.	

Instructions regarding War Diaries and Intelligence Summaries are contained in F. S. Regs., Part II. and the Staff Manual respectively. Title Pages will be prepared in manuscript.

WAR DIARY
or
INTELLIGENCE SUMMARY
(Erase heading not required.)

Army Form C. 2118.

Place	Date	Hour	Summary of Events and Information	Remarks and references to Appendices

Remaining May 31	Admitted	Cured	Evacuated	Died	Destroyed	Remaining under treatment
193	513	393	111	~~7~~ 11	~~7~~ 9	182

The monthly incidence of Contagious disease was as follows. Mange 4. 5. 5. 3 10 = 27
Cellulitis. 3. 4. 3. 1 4 = 15

<u>Mortality</u> Horses were destroyed for the following reasons. Fractures 5. Wounds 3
disease 1. Total 9.
Horses died as a result of Colic 10. disease 1. Total 11.

J. J. Holmes Maj AVC
ADVS 5th Cav Div

2449 Wt. W14957/M90 750,000 1/16 J.B.C. & A. Forms/C.2118/12.

Army Form C. 2118.

Instructions regarding War Diaries and Intelligence Summaries are contained in F. S. Regs., Part II. and the Staff Manual respectively. Title Pages will be prepared in manuscript.

WAR DIARY
or
INTELLIGENCE SUMMARY

(Erase heading not required.)

ADVS 5th Cavalry Division

Place	Date	Hour	Summary of Events and Information	Remarks and references to Appendices
July June	1917			
	1st to 12th		Absent in United Kingdom on ordinary leave	
	13th		Inspection A Canadian Mobile Section Ammunition Column & Reserve Park	
	14th		Inspection Divisional Hdqrs. Captain L GOGARTY under orders for duty with Cavalry Corps headquarters	
	15th		Inspection Fort Garry Horse & Lord Strathcona Horse - all [illegible] in [illegible] condition	
	16th		Inspection Secunderabad Cavalry Bde by Divisional Commander	
	19th		Inspection A & B Batteries RCHA wagon lines also Canadian Field Ambulance	
	20th		Inspection Ambala Cavalry Bde by Divisional Commander - Inspection M.G.S. Ambala Cavalry Bde	
	21st		Remounts arrived at [illegible] & DDVS cast unsuitable horses.	

2449 Wt. W14957/M90 750,000 1/16 J.B.C. & A. Forms/C.2118/12.

Army Form C. 2118.

WAR DIARY
or
INTELLIGENCE SUMMARY
(Erase heading not required.)

Instructions regarding War Diaries and Intelligence Summaries are contained in F. S. Regs., Part II. and the Staff Manual respectively. Title Pages will be prepared in manuscript.

Place	Date	Hour	Summary of Events and Information	Remarks and references to Appendices
Field June	22		Placed on sick in quarters list on account of boils	
	26th		Made arrangement for applying mallein test to horses of Ammunition Column (RHA & RGA) owing to detection of case of Glanders from this unit at the base –	
	29th		Inspection of horses of Div Headquarters Reserve Park & [illegible] Coy by Div Commander	
	30th		Taken off sick in quarters list	
			From 22.6.17 to 30.6.17 only office work & occasional duties could be performed by me & I was unable to obtain a substitute [illegible] or ADVS	
			A monthly wastage summary is given overleaf	

2449 Wt. W14957/M90 750,000 1/16 J.B.C. & A. Forms/C.2118/12.

Instructions regarding War Diaries and Intelligence Summaries are contained in F. S. Regs., Part II. and the Staff Manual respectively. Title Pages will be prepared in manuscript.

WAR DIARY
or
INTELLIGENCE SUMMARY
(Erase heading not required.)

Army Form C. 2118.

Place	Date	Hour	Summary of Events and Information	Remarks and references to Appendices

Remaining Aug 31	Admitted	Cured	Evacuated	Died	Destroyed	Remaining on hand
193	513	393	111	~~7~~ 11	~~#~~ 9	182

The weekly incidence of contagious disease was as follows. Mange 4 5 5 3 10 = 27

Cellulitis. 3 4 3 1 4 = 15

Mortality Horses were destroyed for the following reasons. Fractures 5. Wounds 3

Disease 1 Total 9.

Horses died as a result of Colic 10 disease 1. Total 11.

[illegible] Maj AVC
ADVS 5th Can Div

2449 Wt. W14957/M90 750,000 1/16 J.B.C. & A. Forms/C.2118/12.

Instructions regarding War Diaries and Intelligence Summaries are contained in F. S. Regs., Part II. and the Staff Manual respectively. Title Pages will be prepared in manuscript.

WAR DIARY
or
INTELLIGENCE SUMMARY
(Erase heading not required.)

Army Form C. 2118.

A.D.V.S. 5th Cavalry Division

Place	Date	Hour	Summary of Events and Information	Remarks and references to Appendices
	JULY.			
NOBESCOURT FARM	1st to 9th		Office work. Visited Cavalry Corps Headquarters daily	
"	10th		Moved to BOUVINCOURT Arrived 11 AM.	
BOUVINCOURT	11th		Office work.	
"	12th		Conference of Divisional Veterinary Officers at Divisional Headquarters	
"	13th		Captain H.B. Collet A.V.C. instructed to act as A.D.V.S. of Division. A.D.V.S. joined Corps H.Q. (a/D.D.V.S.)	
"	14th		Commenced march to St POL.	
	15th – 16th		On the march.	
	17th		Arrived at St POL 2 AM	
ST POL.	18th – 19th		Office work	
"	20th		Horses of 17th Brigade R.H.A. inspected.	
"	21st – 30th		Office work	
"	31st		Conference of ADs VS Cavalry Divisions at Cavalry Corps Headquarters	H Saunders Capt AVC a/ADVS 5th Cav Div
			A Wastage Summary for the month is attached	

2449 Wt. W14957/M90 750,000 1/16 J.B.C. & A. Forms/C.2118/12.

Monthly Wastage Summary.

REMAINING JUNE 30th	ADMITTED	CURED	EVACUATED	DIED	DESTROYED	REMAINING
182	490	332	150	7	13	170

DIED

Intussusception	1
Enteritis	2
Rupture of Stomach	2
Impaction of intestine	1
Septicaemia	1
	7

DESTROYED

Tetanus	1
P. U. N.	1
Ulcerative Cellulitis	1
Wound lacerated. Open joint.	1
Fractured tibia	2
" radius	2
" metacarpus	3
Pneumonia	1
Calculus	1
	13

Monthly Wastage Summary.

REMAINING JUNE 30th	ADMITTED	CURED	EVACUATED	DIED	DESTROYED	REMAINING
182	490	332	150	7	13	170

DIED

Intussusception	1
Enteritis	2
Rupture of Stomach	2
Impaction of intestine	1
Septicaemia	1
	7

DESTROYED

Tetanus	1
P. U. N.	1
Ulcerative Cellulitis	1
Wound lacerated. Open joint.	1
Fractured tibia	2
radius	2
metacarpus	3
Pneumonia	1
Calculus	1
	13

Copy of War Diary for the month of July 1917

Place	Date	
NOBESCOURT FM.	1st to 9th	Office work. Daily visit to Cav. Corps. HdQrs.
"	10th	Moved to BOUVINCOURT. Arrived 11 AM.
BOUVINCOURT	11th	Office work
"	12th	Held Conference of Divisional Veterinary Officers.
"	13th	Captain Collet, AVC. M.V.S. Sec'bad Cav. Bde instructed to act as A.D.V.S. of Division. A.D.V.S. joined Cavalry Corps HdQrs.
"	14th	Commenced march to St POL.
	15th - 16th	On the march.
	17th	Arrived at St POL 2 PM.
ST. POL.	18th - 19th	Office work.
"	20th	Horses of 17th Bde R.H.A. inspected.
"	21st to 30th	Office work.
"	31st	Attended Conference of A.D.V.S. Cavalry Divisions at D.D.V.S. Cavalry Corps. HdQrs

Monthly Wastage Summary attached

Instructions regarding War Diaries and Intelligence Summaries are contained in F. S. Regs., Part II. and the Staff Manual respectively. Title Pages will be prepared in manuscript.

WAR DIARY
or
INTELLIGENCE SUMMARY

(Erase heading not required.)

Army Form C. 2118.

A.D.V.S 5th Cavalry Division

Place	Date	Hour	Summary of Events and Information	Remarks and references to Appendices
Divl Hdqrs	August 1st		Captain P.T. Saunders A.V.C took over the duties of A.D.V.S from Captain H.B. COLLET A.V.C	
	"	17th	Captain W.F. TOWILL A.V.C. (Canadian) reported his arrival for duty with Canadian Cavalry Brigade.	
	"	18th	Cavalry Corps Commander inspected Canadian Cavalry Brigade.	
	"	22nd	Major H.J. Stoxness took over duties of A.D.V.S 5th Cav Division on relinquishing the appointment of acting D.D.V.S Cavalry Corps.	
	"	23rd	Inspected M.V. Section of the Division	
	"	24th	Inspected horses of Divisional Hdqrs. Evacuated five horses, two mange, three ordinary cases.	
	"	25th	D.D.V.S Cavalry Corps inspected M.V.S. Ambala & Secunderabad Cavalry Brigades also Canadian Machine Gun Squadron.	

2449 Wt. W14957/M90 750,000 1/16 J.B.C. & A. Forms/C.2118/12.

Instructions regarding War Diaries and Intelligence Summaries are contained in F. S. Regs., Part II. and the Staff Manual respectively. Title Pages will be prepared in manuscript.

WAR DIARY
or
INTELLIGENCE SUMMARY
(Erase heading not required.)

Army Form C. 2118.

Place	Date	Hour	Summary of Events and Information	Remarks and references to Appendices
August	27th		D.D.R. Cavalry Corps inspected Mares of Divisional Headquarters & Lucknow Cavalry Bde with a view to selecting Brood Mares. He selected 2 in Headquarters & 4 in Lucknow Brigade.	
	28th		Inspection of Regimental sick Canadian M.G. Squadron & R.C. Dragoons.	
	29th		D.D.R. inspected Mares of Ambala Cavalry Brigade – selected 20 Mares for registration as Brood Mares.	
	30th		D.D.R. inspected Mares of Canadian Cavalry Brigade, Auxilliary H.T. Coy & Reserve Park & selected seven for registration.	
	31st		122 Remounts arrived at Railhead for the division – train five hours late in arriving	
			A table of Veterinary Casualties for the month of ~~[illegible]~~ August is attached. [illegible]	

2449 Wt. W14957/M90 750,000 1/16 J.B.C. & A. Forms/C.2118/12.

Army Form C. 2118.

Instructions regarding War Diaries and Intelligence Summaries are contained in F. S. Regs., Part II. and the Staff Manual respectively. Title Pages will be prepared in manuscript.

WAR DIARY
or
INTELLIGENCE SUMMARY

(Erase heading not required.)

Place	Date	Hour	Summary of Events and Information	Remarks and references to Appendices

Remaining 31.7.17	Admissions	Cured	Evacuated	Died	Discharged	Remaining 31.7.17
170	504	399	93	6	6	170

L. J. Holmes Maj AVC
ADVS 5th Cav Div

2449 Wt. W14957/M90 750,000 1/16 J.B.C. & A. Forms/C.2118/12.

Instructions regarding War Diaries and Intelligence Summaries are contained in F. S. Regs., Part II. and the Staff Manual respectively. Title Pages will be prepared in manuscript.

WAR DIARY
or
INTELLIGENCE SUMMARY
(Erase heading not required.)

Army Form C. 2118.

A.D.V.S. 5th Cavalry Division

Place	Date	Hour	Summary of Events and Information	Remarks and references to Appendices
Div^l H^d Q^rs	August 1st		Captain P. T. Saunders A.V.C took over the duties of A.D.V.S from Captain H. B. COLLET A.V.C	
	17th		Captain W. F. TOWILL A.V.C. (Canadian) reported his arrival for duty with Canadian Cavalry Brigade.	
	" 18th		Cavalry Corps Commander inspected Canadian Cavalry Brigade.	
	" 22nd		Major H. J. [illegible] took over duties of ADVS 5th Cav Division on relinquishing the appointment of acting DDVS Cavalry Corps.	
	" 23rd		Inspected M.V. Section of the Division	
	" 24th		Inspected horses of Divisional HdQrs [illegible] from [illegible] three [illegible] cases.	
	" 25th		DDVS Cavalry Corps inspected M.V.S. Ambala & Secbad Cavalry Brigades also Canadian Machine Gun Squadron	

2449 Wt. W14957/M90 750,000 1/16 J.B.C. & A. Forms/C.2118/12.

Army Form C. 2118.

WAR DIARY
or
INTELLIGENCE SUMMARY
(Erase heading not required.)

Instructions regarding War Diaries and Intelligence Summaries are contained in F. S. Regs., Part II. and the Staff Manual respectively. Title Pages will be prepared in manuscript.

Place	Date	Hour	Summary of Events and Information	Remarks and references to Appendices
August	27th		D.D.R. Cavalry Corps inspected horses of Divisional Headquarters & [illegible] Cavalry Bde with a view to selecting Brood Mares. He selected [illegible] Headquarters & 4 in Canadian [illegible] Brigade.	
	28th		Inspection of Regimental sick Canadian M.G. Squadron & R.C. Dragoons	
	29th		D.D.R. inspected horses of Ambala Cavalry Brigade – selected 20 mares for registration as brood mares.	
	30th		D.D.R. inspected horses of Canadian Cavalry Brigade, Ammunition?, H.T. Coy & Remount Park & selected seven for registration.	
	31st		122 Remounts arrived at Railhead for the division – train five hours late in arriving	
			A table of Veterinary [illegible] for the month of ~~September~~ August is attached.	

2449 Wt. W14957/M90 750,000 1/16 J.B.C. & A. Forms/C.2118/12.

Instructions regarding War Diaries and Intelligence Summaries are contained in F. S. Regs., Part II. and the Staff Manual respectively. Title Pages will be prepared in manuscript.

WAR DIARY
or
INTELLIGENCE SUMMARY
(Erase heading not required.)

Army Form C. 2118.

Place	Date	Hour	Summary of Events and Information	Remarks and references to Appendices

Remaining 31.7.17	Admissions	Cured	Evacuated	Died	Destroyed	Remaining 31.7.17
170	504	399	93	6	6	170

H. J. Holmes Maj AVC
ADVS 5th Cav Divn

2449 Wt. W14957/M90 750,000 1/16 J.B.C. & A. Forms/C.2118/12.

Instructions regarding War Diaries and Intelligence Summaries are contained in F. S. Regs., Part II. and the Staff Manual respectively. Title Pages will be prepared in manuscript.

WAR DIARY
or
INTELLIGENCE SUMMARY
(*Erase heading not required.*)

A.D.V.S. 5th Cavy Divn.

ADVS 5th Cavalry Division

Army Form C. 2118.

Serial No. 9.

Place	Date	Hour	Summary of Events and Information	Remarks and references to Appendices
September	1.		Cavalry Corps Horse Show.	
	2nd		Office routine. Visited Secunderabad Cavalry Bde Mobile Vety Section.	
	3rd		Inspection all horses VIII K.R.I. Hussars. arranged evacuation of 9 horses, visited regimental sick lines 19 Lancers & 16th M.G. Squadron	
	4th		D.D.V.S. Cavalry Corps inspected M.V. Section this division.	
	5th		Inspected horses of M.M.P & Stages A.S.C	
	6th		Inspected Regimental sick cases Secunderabad Brigade, also A Squadron 7th D.G. & M.G. Squadron	
	7th		Inspected Regimental sick Fort Garry Horse, arranged redistribution of chargers in Canadian Cavalry Brigade	
	9th		Inspected M.V.S. "A" Canadian Cavalry Bde	
	10th		Inspected A Battery R.C.H.A. - horses on the whole poor arranged evacuation of 35 for debility	

2449 Wt. W14957/M90 750,000 1/16 J.B.C. & A. Forms/C.2118/12.

Instructions regarding War Diaries and Intelligence Summaries are contained in F. S. Regs., Part II. and the Staff Manual respectively. Title Pages will be prepared in manuscript.

WAR DIARY
or
INTELLIGENCE SUMMARY
(Erase heading not required.)

Army Form C. 2118.

Place	Date	Hour	Summary of Events and Information	Remarks and references to Appendices
September	11th		Inspection N Battery RHA & B Battery RCHA	
	13th		GOC RHA Cavalry Corps, DDR & DDVS inspected horses of RHA & RCHA units several classified unsuitable & ~~…~~ on 90 cast on veterinary grounds.	
	14th		Re inspection A & B Batteries RCHA arranged evacuation of 48 & 37 horses respectively	
	19th		Inspection Regimental units & horses L. S. H., fine units - horses in good condition	
	21st		DDVS Cavalry Corps inspected M. V. S. of the division	
	23rd		Inspection M.V.S. Artillery Brigade & Regimental units of the Horse & X Battery also Reserve Park	
	25th		Captain M.G. O'Fogarty C. AVC reported his arrival & was appointed O.C. M.V.S. A Canadian Cavalry Bde & V.O. R.C.D.	
			Captain Sheeran C. AVC posted to R.C.H.A. & M.G.S. from M.V.S. A.	

2449 Wt. W14957/M90 750,000 1/16 J.B.C. & A. Forms/C.2118/12.

Instructions regarding War Diaries and Intelligence Summaries are contained in F. S. Regs., Part II. and the Staff Manual respectively. Title Pages will be prepared in manuscript.

WAR DIARY
or
INTELLIGENCE SUMMARY
(Erase heading not required.)

Army Form C. 2118.

Place	Date	Hour	Summary of Events and Information	Remarks and references to Appendices
September	27th		Inspected chargers Officers [illegible] board on horses RCHA resulting in one [illegible] horse being handed to A.R. Depot – Captain Heenan CAVC detailed to proceed with the party	
			Lt. WARNEFORD explained arrangement of Ring Road.	
	28		Inspected horses of Signal Squadron & Cavalry Field Ambulance.	
	29		Inspected Canadian M.V. Section & horses for evacuation	
	30		Inspected Ambulance M.V. Section also X Battery and Ammunition Column 17th Bde RHA & RCHA Brigade	
			Routine duties were carried out on days not otherwise mentioned	
			Summary of [illegible] attached	

2449 Wt. W14957/M90 750,000 1/16 J.B.C. & A. Forms/C.2118/12.

Army Form C. 2118.

Instructions regarding War Diaries and Intelligence Summaries are contained in F. S. Regs., Part II. and the Staff Manual respectively. Title Pages will be prepared in manuscript.

WAR DIARY
or
INTELLIGENCE SUMMARY
(Erase heading not required.)

Place	Date	Hour	Summary of Events and Information	Remarks and references to Appendices

Veterinary hospital for month of September 1917

Remaining	admitted	Cured	evacuated	died	destroyed	Remaining
170	540	293	251	5	11	150.

V. J. Holmes Maj AVC
A.D.V.S. Vth Cav Div

2449 Wt. W14957/M90 750,000 1/16 J.B.C. & A. Forms/C.2118/12.

Instructions regarding War Diaries and Intelligence Summaries are contained in F. S. Regs., Part II. and the Staff Manual respectively. Title Pages will be prepared in manuscript.

WAR DIARY
or
INTELLIGENCE SUMMARY
(Erase heading not required.)

ADVS 5th Cavalry Division

Army Form C. 2118.

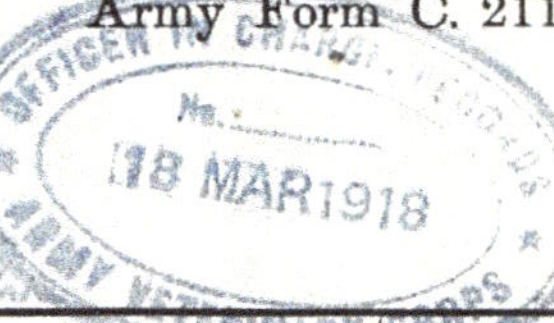

Place	Date	Hour	Summary of Events and Information	Remarks and references to Appendices
September	1		Cavalry Corps Horse Show	
	2nd		Office routine. Visited Lucknow Cavalry Bde Mobile Vety Section	
	3rd		Inspection all horses VIII KRI Hussars arranged evacuation of 9 horses, inspected Regimental sick 18 Lancers & M.G. Squadron	
	4th		DDVS Cavalry Corps inspected M.V. Sections the division.	
	5th		Inspected horses of M.M.P. & [illegible] ASC	
	6th		Inspected Regimental sick cases Lucknow Brigade also A Squadron 7th D.G. & M.G. Squadron	
	7th		Inspected Regimental sick Fort Garry Horse arranged redistribution of [illegible] in Canadian Cavalry Brigade	
	9th		Inspection M.V.S. Canadian Cavalry Bde	
	10th		Inspection A Battery R.C.H.A. – horses on the whole poor arranged evacuation of 35 for debility	

2449 Wt. W14957/M90 750,000 1/16 J.B.C. & A. Forms/C.2118/12.

Army Form C. 2118.

WAR DIARY
or
INTELLIGENCE SUMMARY
(Erase heading not required.)

Instructions regarding War Diaries and Intelligence Summaries are contained in F. S. Regs., Part II. and the Staff Manual respectively. Title Pages will be prepared in manuscript.

Place	Date	Hour	Summary of Events and Information	Remarks and references to Appendices
September	11th		Inspected N Battery RHA & B Battery RCHA	
	13th		GOC RHA Cavalry Corps DDR & DDVS inspected horses of RHA & RCHA with several classified unsuitable & [illegible] 90 cast as being [illegible]	
	14th		The inspection A & B Batteries RCHA arranged evacuation of 48 & 37 horses respectively	
	19th		Inspected Regimental sick & horses L.S.H. few sick – horses in good condition	
	21st		DDVS Cavalry Corps inspected M.V.S. of the division	
	23rd		Inspected M.V.S. Attached Brigade & Regimental sick 9th Horse & X Battery also Reserve Park	
	25th		Captain McE O'Gogarty C AVC reported his arrival & was attached OC M.V.S. A Canadian Cavalry Bde & 6 O/C R.C.D.	
			Captain Heanan C AVC posted to RCHA & M.G.S. from M.V.S. A	

2449 Wt. W14957/M90 750,000 1/16 J.B.C. & A. Forms/C.2118/12.

Instructions regarding War Diaries and Intelligence Summaries are contained in F. S. Regs., Part II. and the Staff Manual respectively. Title Pages will be prepared in manuscript.

WAR DIARY
or
INTELLIGENCE SUMMARY

(Erase heading not required.)

Army Form C. 2118.

Place	Date	Hour	Summary of Events and Information	Remarks and references to Appendices
September	27th		Inspected charges [illegible] [illegible] found in horses RCHA resulting in two [illegible] horses being handed to A.R. Depot - Captain [illegible] CAVC detailed to proceed with the party	
			At WARNEFORD explain arrangements of [illegible] lines	
	28		Inspected horses of Signal Squadron & Cavalry Field Ambulance.	
	29		Inspected [illegible] M.V. Section & horses for [illegible]	
	30		Inspected Ambulance M.V. Section also X Battery and Ammunition Column 17th Bde RHA & RCHA Brigade	
			Routine duties were carried out as charges and [illegible]	
			Summary of [illegible] attached	

2449 Wt. W14957/M90 750,000 1/16 J.B.C. & A. Forms/C.2118/12.

Army Form C. 2118.

Instructions regarding War Diaries and Intelligence Summaries are contained in F. S. Regs., Part II. and the Staff Manual respectively. Title Pages will be prepared in manuscript.

WAR DIARY
or
INTELLIGENCE SUMMARY
(Erase heading not required.)

Place	Date	Hour	Summary of Events and Information	Remarks and references to Appendices
			Veterinary [illegible] for month of September 1917	

Remaining	admitted	Cured	evacuated	died	destroyed	Remaining
170	540	293	251	5	11	150

V.L.J. [illegible] Maj AVC
A.D.V.S. V Cav Div

2449 Wt. W14957/M90 750,000 1/16 J.B.C. & A. Forms/C.2118/12.

Instructions regarding War Diaries and Intelligence Summaries are contained in F. S. Regs., Part II. and the Staff Manual respectively. Title Pages will be prepared in manuscript.

WAR DIARY
or
INTELLIGENCE SUMMARY
(Erase heading not required.)

Army Form C. 2118.

9.

A.D.V.S. 5th Cavalry Division

Place	Date	Hour	Summary of Events and Information	Remarks and references to Appendices
1917. October	1st		Inspection horses L.S.H. and A Battery R.C.H.A. orders received re [illegible] [illegible] lost to X Battery R.H.A.	
	2nd		D.D.R. Cavalry Corps selected horses for casting for other than Veterinary reasons.	
	3		All horses X Battery with Ammunition Column X section passed [illegible] test	
	5		Orders received for the Division to march North. arranged evacuation of cases cast by D.D.R.	
	6		Canadian & Secunderabad Brigades marched to WATOU. POPERINGHE area. Weather changed - wet & cold.	
	7		Proceeded to new area by car - visited D.D.V.S. Cavalry Corps en route to POPERINGHE	
	8th		Visited A.D.V.S. IInd Anzac Corps met D.D.V.S. II Army arranged method of evacuating horses from II Army area	
	9		Visited A M.V.S. Canadian Cavalry Bde explained evacuation measures & [illegible] [illegible] condition.	

2449 Wt. W14957/M90 750,000 1/16 J.B.C. & A. Forms/C.2118/12.

Instructions regarding War Diaries and Intelligence Summaries are contained in F. S. Regs., Part II. and the Staff Manual respectively. Title Pages will be prepared in manuscript.

WAR DIARY
or
INTELLIGENCE SUMMARY
(Erase heading not required.)

Army Form C. 2118.

Place	Date	Hour	Summary of Events and Information	Remarks and references to Appendices
Octr	10th		Visited Commandant MVS explained principle of evacuation in 3rd Army area & line of [illegible] during operation.	
	11th		Inspected RCHA Canadian M.G. Squadron & A.H.T. Company.	
	13th		Lieutenant MAGUIRE AVC V.O. [illegible] called at office & received instructions. Inspected Ambala M.V.S. Orders to march South received.	
	14th		Marched to ATTERES CURE	
	16th		Marched to FRESSIN area.	
	17th		Proceeded on leave of absence to ENGLAND having arranged for duties to be carried on by Capt [illegible] SHEFFIELD AVC	
	29th		Returned from leave of absence took on duties of ADVS inspected [illegible] M.V.S	
	30		Office routine	
	31		Inspected Ambala M.V.S & arranged for treatment of [illegible].	

2449 Wt. W14957/M90 750,000 1/16 J.B.C. & A. Forms/C.2118/12.

Army Form C. 2118.

Instructions regarding War Diaries and Intelligence Summaries are contained in F. S. Regs., Part II. and the Staff Manual respectively. Title Pages will be prepared in manuscript.

WAR ~~DIARY~~ *or* INTELLIGENCE SUMMARY

(Erase heading not required.)

Place	Date	Hour	Summary of Events and Information	Remarks and references to Appendices
			Veterinary Statistics for month of Octbr 1917	

Remaining	Admissions in Octbr	Cured	Evacuated	Died	Destroyed	Remaining	
150	477	333	93	8	10	183.	

J. J. Holmes Maj AVC
ADVS 5th Cav Div

2449 Wt. W14957/M90 750,000 1/16 J.B.C. & A. Forms/C.2118/12.

Instructions regarding War Diaries and Intelligence Summaries are contained in F. S. Regs., Part II. and the Staff Manual respectively. Title Pages will be prepared in manuscript.

WAR DIARY
or
INTELLIGENCE SUMMARY

(Erase heading not required.)

Army Form C. 2118.

ADVS 5th Cavalry Divn

Place	Date	Hour	Summary of Events and Information	Remarks and references to Appendices
1917 Feb	1st		Inspection horses L.S.H. and A Battery, R.C.H.A. [illegible] [illegible] [illegible] [illegible] [illegible] to X Battery RCHA	
	2nd		D.D.R. Cavalry Corps [illegible] horses for [illegible] [illegible] [illegible] Veterinary [illegible]	
	3		All horses X Battery with Ammunition Column X section [illegible] Battery [illegible]	
	5		[illegible] [illegible] for the [illegible] [illegible] [illegible] arranged [illegible] of [illegible] [illegible] by DDR	
	6		Canadian & Secunderabad Brigades marched to WATOU POPERINGHE area. Weather changed - very cold	
	7		[illegible] [illegible] area by car. Visited DDVS Cavalry Corps en route to POPERINGHE	
	8th		Visited ADVS II Anzac Corps met DDVS II Army arranged method of evacuating horses from II Army area	
	9		Visited A.D.V.S. Canadian Cavalry Bde explaining evacuation [illegible] & field [illegible] conditions	

2449 Wt. W14957/M90 750,000 1/16 J.B.C. & A. Forms/C.2118/12.

Instructions regarding War Diaries and Intelligence Summaries are contained in F. S. Regs., Part II. and the Staff Manual respectively. Title Pages will be prepared in manuscript.

WAR DIARY
or
INTELLIGENCE SUMMARY
(Erase heading not required.)

Army Form C. 2118.

Place	Date	Hour	Summary of Events and Information	Remarks and references to Appendices
Octr	10th		Visited [illegible] MVS [illegible] [illegible] 5th Army [illegible] line of [illegible] during operations	
	11th		Inspected RCHA Canadian MG Squadron & ANT Company	
	13th		Lieutenant MAGUIRE AVC [illegible] [illegible] called at office re [illegible]	
			Inspected Ambala MVS [illegible] to [illegible] South [illegible]	
	14th		Marched to TREAESCURE	
	16th		Marched to FRESSIN area	
	17th		Proceeded on leave of absence to ENGLAND having arranged for duties of the Command [illegible] Capt W L SHEFFIELD AVC	
	29th		Returned from leave of absence [illegible] duties of ADVS [illegible] Sec Bde MVS	
	30		Office routine	
	31		Inspected Ambala MVS & arranged for [illegible] of [illegible]	

Army Form C. 2118.

Instructions regarding War Diaries and Intelligence Summaries are contained in F. S. Regs., Part II. and the Staff Manual respectively. Title Pages will be prepared in manuscript.

WAR DIARY
or
INTELLIGENCE SUMMARY
(Erase heading not required.)

Place	Date	Hour	Summary of Events and Information	Remarks and references to Appendices
			Veterinary [illegible] for month of October 1917	

Remaining	admission sick	cured	evacuated	died	destroyed	Remaining
150	477	333	93	8	10	183

S.J. Stokes Maj AVC
ADVS 5th Cav Div

2449 Wt. W14957/M90 750,000 1/16 J.B.C. & A. Forms/C.2118/12.

Instructions regarding War Diaries and Intelligence Summaries are contained in F. S. Regs., Part II. and the Staff Manual respectively. Title pages will be prepared in manuscript.

WAR DIARY
or
INTELLIGENCE SUMMARY.
(*Erase heading not required.*)

Army Form C. 2118.

9

A.D.V.S. V[th] Cavalry Division

Place	Date	Hour	Summary of Events and Information	Remarks and references to Appendices
	1917			
November	1st		Inspection horses Divisional Hqrs. ASC & MMP	
	3		Divisional Commander inspection the horses of the Division. Inspected M.V.S. A Canadian Cavalry Bde	
	5th		D.D.V.S. Cavalry Corps inspected M.V.S. A Canadian Cavalry Bde	
	7th		Inspected M.V.S. Ambala Cavalry Bde & Right units Ambala Bde	
	8th		Inspection M.V.S. [illegible] Bde, Captain O'Fogarty C.AVC under orders to proceed for duty to England	
	9th		Division under orders to march.	
	10.11.12		Division marched to BOUVINCOURT area via DOULLENS QUERRIEU	
	13		Inspected Vety arrangements Ambala Bde Captain DUNHOLT C.AVC reported for duty with M.V.S. A	
	14		Inspected Vety arrangements [illegible] Bde – Captain O'FOGARTY left the Division [illegible]	
	16		Visited Canadian M.V.S. saw evacuation cases.	
	17		Conference at office of DDVS re possible operations also conference of OC M.V.S. 5th Cav Div	
	18		Conference of Vety Officers 5th Cav Divn regarding movement in the event of operations	
	19		Marched 1.30 AM to FINS area with Hq Echelon D.Hqrs	
	21		Marched 6.30 AM to VILLERS PLUICH & joined divisional concentration	

2353 Wt. W2544/1454 700,000 5/15 D. D. & L. A.D.S.S./Forms/C. 2118.

Instructions regarding War Diaries and Intelligence Summaries are contained in F. S. Regs., Part II. and the Staff Manual respectively. Title pages will be prepared in manuscript.

WAR DIARY
or
INTELLIGENCE SUMMARY.
(Erase heading not required.)

Army Form C. 2118.

Place	Date	Hour	Summary of Events and Information	Remarks and references to Appendices
[illegible]	22		Marched to EQUANCOURT	
	23		March to SUZANNE	
	24		Ordered by G.O.C to ascertain horse deficiencies in the Division – deficient 393	
	26		Inspected M.V. Section Artillery & [illegible] Brigade	
	27		Marched to MONCHY LAGACHE	
	28		Remounts arrived at Railhead [illegible] disembarkation division concentrated in neighbourhood of EPEHY	
	29		Joined A2 echelon arranged [illegible] of M.V.S. & [illegible] personnel	
	30		Remained with A2 Echelon	

Horse history during November 1917

Remaining Oct 31	Admissions	Cured	Evacuated	Died & Killed in action		Destroyed	Remaining
183	922	500	200	151	[illegible]	12	142

J. Holmes Maj AVC
ADVS 5th Cav Div

2353 Wt. W2544/1454 700,000 5/15 D. D. & L. A.D.S.S./Forms/C. 2118.

Army Form C. 2118.

WAR DIARY
or
INTELLIGENCE SUMMARY.
(Erase heading not required.)

Instructions regarding War Diaries and Intelligence Summaries are contained in F. S. Regs., Part II. and the Staff Manual respectively. Title pages will be prepared in manuscript.

A.D.V.S. Vth Cavalry Division

Place	Date	Hour	Summary of Events and Information	Remarks and references to Appendices
	1917			
November	1st		Inspection horses Divisional Hqrs. ASC & MMP	
	3		Divisional Commander inspected the horses of the Division. Inspected M.V.S. & Canadian Cavalry Bde	
	5th		D.D.V.S. Cavalry Corps inspected M.V.S. & Canadian Cavalry Bde	
	7th		Inspected M.V.S. Ambala Cavalry Bde – [illegible] Ambala Bde	
	8th		Inspection M.V.S. Sec Bad Captain [illegible] under orders to proceed for duty in England.	
	9th		Division under orders to march.	
	10. 11. 12		Division marched to BOUVINCOURT area via DOULLENS QUERRIEU	
	13		Inspected Vety arrangements Ambala Bde Captain DUNHOLT [illegible] for duty with	M.V.S. [illegible]
	14		Inspected Vety arrangements Sec Bad – Captain O'GARTY [illegible]	
	16		Visited Canadian M.V.S. saw [illegible] cases.	
	17		Conference at office of D.D.V.S. on possible operations. Also conference of O.C. M.V.S. 5th Cav Div	
	18		Conference of Vety officers 5th Cav Div regarding movement in the event of operations	
	19		Marched 1.30 AM to FINS area with A. Echelon D Hqrs	
	21		Marched 6.30 AM to VILLERS PLOUICH to form divisional [illegible]	

2353 Wt. W2544/1454 700,000 5/15 D. D. & L. A.D.S.S./Forms/C. 2118.

Instructions regarding War Diaries and Intelligence Summaries are contained in F. S. Regs., Part II. and the Staff Manual respectively. Title pages will be prepared in manuscript.

WAR DIARY
or
INTELLIGENCE SUMMARY.
(Erase heading not required.)

Army Form C. 2118.

Place	Date	Hour	Summary of Events and Information	Remarks and references to Appendices
Tincourt	22		Marched to EQUANCOURT	
	23		Marched to SUZANNE	
	24		Orders by G.O.C. to ascertain horse deficiencies in the Division – deficient 393	
	26		Inspected M.V. Section Artillery & Cavalry Brigade	
	27		Marched to MONCHY LAGACHE	
	28		Remounts arrived at Railhead attended detrainment [illegible] Division [illegible] YEPESY?	
	29		Joined A2 Echelon arranged employment of M.V.S. & Vets personnel	
	30		Remained with A2 Echelon	

Horse wastage during November 1917.

Remaining Oct 31	Admissions	Cured	Evacuated	Died Killed in action		Destroyed	Remaining
153	922	500	300	131	[illegible]	12	132

[illegible] Major [illegible]
A.D.V.S. 5th Cav Div.

2353 Wt. W2544/1454 700,000 5/15 D. D. & L. A.D.S.S./Forms/C. 2118.

Instructions regarding War Diaries and Intelligence Summaries are contained in F. S. Regs., Part II. and the Staff Manual respectively. Title Pages will be prepared in manuscript.

WAR DIARY
or
INTELLIGENCE SUMMARY
(Erase heading not required.)

A.D.V.S. 5th Cav Div

Army Form C. 2118.

(9)

Place	Date	Hour	Summary of Events and Information	Remarks and references to Appendices
	1.12.17.		Operations round CAMBRAI. M.V. Section with A2 Echelon & detachments attending both to Unit & Brigade Hqrs, bringing in casualties which were shown to M.V.S. 55th Divn at VILLERS FAUCON which was acting as a Veterinary Casualty Clearing station	
	2.12.17		Brigades joined Echelons	
	3.12.17		Divisional Hqrs moved to LONGAVESNES	
	5.12.17		Inspected Ambala M.V. Section saw cases for treatment	
	6.12.17		Inspected Canadian M.V. Section	
	7.12.17		Inspected Secunderabad M.V. Section	
	8.12.17		Divl Hqrs Ambala & Secunderabad Bdes moved to CARTIGNY – MONCHY LAGACHE area	
	9.12.17		Visited Ambala & Secunderabad Brigade area.	
	11.12.17		Conference of all Veterinary Officers regarding the recent operation & the lessons for dealing with	

2449 Wt. W14957/M90 750,000 1/16 J.B.C. & A. Forms/C.2118/12.

Army Form C. 2118.

WAR DIARY
or
INTELLIGENCE SUMMARY
(Erase heading not required.)

Instructions regarding War Diaries and Intelligence Summaries are contained in F. S. Regs., Part II. and the Staff Manual respectively. Title Pages will be prepared in manuscript.

Place	Date	Hour	Summary of Events and Information	Remarks and references to Appendices
			Veterinary Canadian	
	12.12.17		Inspected horses of 17th Bde RHA Ammunition & RCHA Ammunition Col.	
	13.12.17		Inspected horses of Divisional Supply also Artillery Mob. Vet. Section	
	14.12.17		DDVS Cavalry Corps visits division & inspected M.V. Sections	
	15.12.17		Visited OC 2nd Division M.V.S. also inspected horse clipping [illegible] at BEAUMETZ	
	16.12.17		Inspected A & B Batteries RCHA together with [illegible] Ammun Column.	
	17.12.17		Canadian Brigade moves into MERAUCOURT area & [illegible] Brigade into TREFCON area. [illegible] M.V.S. [illegible] for [illegible] with Manège	
	19.12.17		Reinforcements arrive at Railhead	
	20.12.17		Inspected horses of Field Squadron R.E. also [illegible] M.V. Section	

2449 Wt. W14957/M90 750,000 1/16 J.B.C. & A. Forms/C.2118/12.

Instructions regarding War Diaries and Intelligence Summaries are contained in F. S. Regs., Part II. and the Staff Manual respectively. Title Pages will be prepared in manuscript.

WAR DIARY
or
INTELLIGENCE SUMMARY
(Erase heading not required.)

Army Form C. 2118.

Place	Date	Hour	Summary of Events and Information	Remarks and references to Appendices
	21.12.17		Inspection RCHA Ammunition Column in account of Mange occurring among the horses of that unit	
			Inspection ADVS 7th Corps re clipping bath at BEAUMETZ	
	22.12.17		Inspection Mob. of Reserve Park also Supp. ASC Train & horses	
	26.12.17		Inspection MVS Lucknow & Ambala	
	29.12.17		Inspection A. M.V.S. Canadian Brigade	
	30.12.17		Inspection RHA Headquarters also Sialkot Lucknow Bde	
	31.12.17		Ambala M.V.S. converted into a hospital for dealing with all cases of ophthalmia in the division	

Army Form C. 2118.

WAR DIARY
or
INTELLIGENCE SUMMARY

(Erase heading not required.)

Instructions regarding War Diaries and Intelligence Summaries are contained in F. S. Regs., Part II. and the Staff Manual respectively. Title Pages will be prepared in manuscript.

Place	Date	Hour	Summary of Events and Information	Remarks and references to Appendices
			Summary of Veterinary hospital for December 1917	

Remaining	admissions	Cured	evacuated	died	destroyed	Remaining
142	774	348	255	98 x	22 x	193

x includes Battle casualties

Mange has occurred extensively & shows signs of increasing – during the month 45 cases have occurred. Measures to check the disease are hampered by severe weather – the chief units affected are RCHA Ammunition Col RCHA Brigade R.C. Dragoons & Canadian Brigade Hqrs.

[illegible] Holmes Maj. [illegible]
ADVS 5 Cav Div

2449 Wt. W14957/M90 750,000 1/16 J.B.C. & A. Forms/C.2118/12.

Instructions regarding War Diaries and Intelligence Summaries are contained in F. S. Regs., Part II. and the Staff Manual respectively. Title Pages will be prepared in manuscript.

WAR DIARY
or
INTELLIGENCE SUMMARY
(Erase heading not required.)

A.D.V.S. [illegible]

Army Form C. 2118.

Place	Date	Hour	Summary of Events and Information	Remarks and references to Appendices
	1.12.17		Operations round CAMBRAI [illegible]	
			[illegible] Hqrs [illegible]	
			[illegible]	
	2.12.17		[illegible]	
	3.12.17		[illegible] Hqrs moved to [illegible]	
	[illegible]		[illegible]	
			[illegible]	
	7.12.17		[illegible]	
	8.12.17		[illegible] moved to CAMBRAI [illegible] area	
	9.12.17		Visits [illegible] Brigade area	
	11.12.17		Conference of all Veterinary Officers regarding the recent operations [illegible]	

2449 Wt. W14957/M90 750,000 1/16 J.B.C. & A. Forms/C.2118/12.

Instructions regarding War Diaries and Intelligence Summaries are contained in F. S. Regs., Part II. and the Staff Manual respectively. Title Pages will be prepared in manuscript.

WAR DIARY
or
INTELLIGENCE SUMMARY
(Erase heading not required.)

Army Form C. 2118.

Place	Date	Hour	Summary of Events and Information	Remarks and references to Appendices
			Veterinary [illegible]	
	12.12.17		Inspection horses of 17th Bde RHA Ammunition & RCHA Ammunition Col.	
	13.12.17		Inspected horses of [illegible] also Artillery Mob Vet Section	
	14.12.17		ODVS [illegible] Cav. [illegible] & [illegible] MG Section	
	15.12.17		[illegible] 2nd Division MVS also inspected horses [illegible] at BERNAMETZ	
	16.12.17		Inspected A & B Batteries RCHA together with light section Ammunition Column.	
	17.12.17		Canadian Brigade moves to MERAU COURT area & [illegible] Brigade to TREFCON area. [illegible] MVS [illegible] & [illegible] for [illegible] with [illegible].	
	19.12.17		Remounts arrive at Railhead	
	20.12.17		Inspected horses of Field Squadron RE also [illegible] MG Section	

2449 Wt. W14957/M90 750,000 1/16 J.B.C. & A. Forms/C.2118/12.

Instructions regarding War Diaries and Intelligence Summaries are contained in F. S. Regs., Part II. and the Staff Manual respectively. Title Pages will be prepared in manuscript.

WAR DIARY
or
INTELLIGENCE SUMMARY

(Erase heading not required.)

Army Form C. 2118.

Place	Date	Hour	Summary of Events and Information	Remarks and references to Appendices
	19.12.17		Inspected RCHA Ammunition Column on account of [illegible] [illegible] [illegible] [illegible] [illegible] [illegible]	
			Visited ADVS 7th Cav re [illegible] baths at [illegible]	
	22.12.17		Inspected [illegible] of Reserve Park also [illegible] ASC Trucks & horses	
	26.12.17		Visited MVS [illegible] & [illegible]	
	28.12.17		Inspected A M.V.S. Canadian Brigade	
	30.12.17		Inspected RHA Headquarters also [illegible] [illegible] [illegible]	
	31.12.17		[illegible] M.V.S. [illegible] [illegible] [illegible] for dealing with all cases of [illegible] in the division	

2449 Wt. W14957/M90 750,000 1/16 J.B.C. & A. Forms/C.2118/12.

Army Form C. 2118.

WAR DIARY
or
INTELLIGENCE SUMMARY
(Erase heading not required.)

Instructions regarding War Diaries and Intelligence Summaries are contained in F. S. Regs., Part II. and the Staff Manual respectively. Title Pages will be prepared in manuscript.

Place	Date	Hour	Summary of Events and Information	Remarks and references to Appendices

2449 Wt. W14957/M90 750,000 1/16 J.B.C. & A. Forms/C.2118/12.

Army Form C. 2118.

WAR DIARY
or
INTELLIGENCE SUMMARY

(Erase heading not required.)

Instructions regarding War Diaries and Intelligence Summaries are contained in F. S. Regs., Part II. and the Staff Manual respectively. Title Pages will be prepared in manuscript.

Place	Date	Hour	Summary of Events and Information	Remarks and references to Appendices
			Summary of Veterinary work for December 1917	

Remaining	Admitted	Cured	Transferred	Died	Destroyed	Remaining
142	774	328	205	78 x	22 x	102

x includes Battle casualties

Mange has [illegible] [illegible] during the month 45 cases have occurred [illegible] [illegible] [illegible] as [illegible] [illegible] [illegible] — the [illegible] [illegible] on R.C.H.A. Ammunition Col. R.C.H.A. [illegible] R.C. Dragoons & Canadian Brigade Hqrs.

[illegible] Maj. [illegible]
A.V.S. [illegible]

2449 Wt. W14957/M90 750,000 1/16 J.B.C. & A. Forms/C.2118/12.

Instructions regarding War Diaries and Intelligence Summaries are contained in F. S. Regs., Part II. and the Staff Manual respectively. Title pages will be prepared in manuscript.

~~WAR DIARY~~ or INTELLIGENCE SUMMARY.

(*Erase heading not required.*)

Army Form C. 2118.

(9)

January 1918. A.D.V.S. V Cav. Div.

Place	Date	Hour	Summary of Events and Information	Remarks and references to Appendices
	1.		Visited 36th M.V.S (36th Divn) arranged cooperative system of evacuation of sick animals	
	2		Conference of Veterinary Officers on the subject of Mange & Ophthalmia among horses in the divisional area – arranged treatment of all eye cases at [illegible] M.V.S of Mange cases at [illegible] M.V.S operative surgical cases at Canadian M.V.S	
	3		Inspection animals of Remount Park & M.V.S. A	
	4		Inspection horses F.G. Horse & L.S. Horse	
	7		Inspection R.C.H.A ammunition column, arranged staff of Mange [illegible] at [illegible] LAGACHE.	
	10		Inspection 21 & ½ [illegible] Heavy Battery R.G.A also 3rd A.F.A Brigade	
	11		Inspection [illegible] M.V.S saw progress of ophthalmia cases	
	12		Inspection D. [illegible] A.S.C. [illegible]	
	13		Inspection 76 Brigade R.G.A for Mange	
	14		Inspection [illegible] M.V.S met A.D.V.S 4th Cav Divn re unit of dismounted Divn	
	15		Inspection R.C.H.A Ammn Col. also M.V.S [illegible] & [illegible] Brigade	
	16		Attending [illegible] at [illegible] detachment of C.A.V.C personnel [illegible]	
	17		Inspection horses 3rd Brigade R.H.A also 16 Bde R.H.A saw cases under treatment [illegible] consulted G.O.C re Mange	

2353 Wt. W2544/1454 700,000 5/15 D. D. & L. A.D.S.S./Forms/C. 2118.

Instructions regarding War Diaries and Intelligence Summaries are contained in F. S. Regs., Part II. and the Staff Manual respectively. Title pages will be prepared in manuscript.

WAR DIARY
or
INTELLIGENCE SUMMARY.
(*Erase heading not required.*)

Army Form C. 2118.

Place	Date	Hour	Summary of Events and Information	Remarks and references to Appendices
	18.		Inspected RCHA Amn Col & RHA Amn Col.	
	19.		Arranged clipping of horses Amn Col & [illegible] machines at clipping [illegible] at BEAUMETZ.	
	20		Inspected [illegible] sick [illegible] Cav Bde. VIII Hussars XVIII Lancers & M.G. Sqdn.	
	21		Inspected [illegible] sick Remount Park [illegible]	
	22		Inspected M.V.S. 'A' Canadian Cavalry Bde & RCD.	
	23		Inspected M.V.S. [illegible] sick 9th Horse & [illegible]	
	26		Inspected M.V.S. [illegible]	
	27		Inspected [illegible]	
	28		Inspected J & E Batteries RHA 3rd Amn Col also A & B Batteries RCHA	
	29.		Inspected horses XX Deccan Horse	
	30		[illegible] to A.D.V.S. [illegible] Cav Div [illegible] C & K Batteries RHA	
			The days not specified routine duties were performed. A summary of [illegible] for January is attached	

2353 Wt. W2544/1454 700,000 5/15 D. D. & L. A.D.S.S./Forms/C. 2118.

Army Form C. 2118.

Instructions regarding War Diaries and Intelligence Summaries are contained in F. S. Regs., Part II. and the Staff Manual respectively. Title pages will be prepared in manuscript.

WAR DIARY
or
INTELLIGENCE SUMMARY.
(Erase heading not required.)

Place	Date	Hour	Summary of Events and Information							Remarks and references to Appendices
			Remaining	Admitted during	Cured	Evacuated	Died	Destroyed	Remaining	
			193	540	342	148	3	22	218	

[illegible]

[illegible]

Army Form C. 2118.

Instructions regarding War Diaries and Intelligence Summaries are contained in F. S. Regs., Part II. and the Staff Manual respectively. Title pages will be prepared in manuscript.

WAR DIARY
or
INTELLIGENCE SUMMARY.

(Erase heading not required.)

January 1918 A.D.V.S. V [illegible]

Place	Date	Hour	Summary of Events and Information	Remarks and references to Appendices
	1		Visits 36th M.V.S (30th Div) Arranges Cooperative system of evacuation of sick animals	
	2		Conference of Veterinary Officers on the subject of Mange & Ophthalmia occurring [illegible] the Division area — Arranges treatment of all eye cases at [illegible] M.V.S of Mange cases at [illegible] M.V.S experimental surgical cases at [illegible] M.V.S	
	3		Inspects [illegible] of Remount Park & M.V.S. A	
	4		Inspects horses F.G. Horse 1 L.S. Horse	
	8		Inspects R.C.H.A. Ammunition Column Arranges staff of Mange treatment depot at MORCOURT LAGACHE.	
	10		Inspects 1st [illegible] Siege Heavy Battery R.G.A. also 311 R.F.A. Brigade	
	11		Inspects [illegible] M.V.S [illegible] progress of ophthalmia cases	
	12		Inspects [illegible] [illegible] [illegible] [illegible]	
	13		Inspects 76 Brigade R.G.A. for Mange	
	14		Inspects [illegible] M.V.S [illegible] A.D.V.S 4th Cav Div on [illegible] of dismounted [illegible]	
	15		Inspects R.C.H.A. Ammn Col. also M.V.S [illegible] & [illegible] Brigade	
	16		[illegible] [illegible] at [illegible], [illegible] of C.M.C [illegible] [illegible] of [illegible]	
	17		Inspects horses 3rd Brigade R.H.A. also 16 Bde R.H.A. [illegible] [illegible] [illegible] the [illegible] G.O.C. on Mange	

2353 Wt. W2544/1454 700,000 5/15 D. D. & L. A.D.S.S./Forms/C. 2118.

Instructions regarding War Diaries and Intelligence Summaries are contained in F. S. Regs., Part II. and the Staff Manual respectively. Title pages will be prepared in manuscript.

WAR DIARY
or
INTELLIGENCE SUMMARY.
(Erase heading not required.)

Army Form C. 2118.

Place	Date	Hour	Summary of Events and Information	Remarks and references to Appendices
	18.		Inspected RCHA Amm Col & RHA Amm Col.	
	19.		Arranged shifting of [illegible] Amm Col & Mange Cases under treatment at Shifting [illegible] at BEAUMETZ.	
	20		Inspected Regt units Ambulance [illegible]. VIII Hussars XVIII Lancers & M.G. Sqdn.	
	21.		Inspected [illegible] units Remount Park A.H.T. R.E.	
	22		Inspected M.G.B. [illegible] Canadian Cavalry [illegible] & R.C.D.	
	23		Inspected M.V.S. Ambulance Regt units 9th Hussars & [illegible]	
	26		Inspected M.V.S. Section re list of [illegible]	
	27		Inspected [illegible] [illegible]	
	28		Inspected J & E Batteries RHA 3rd Amm Col also A & B Batteries RCHA.	
	29.		Inspected [illegible] X & Deccan Horse	
	30		[illegible] [illegible] to ADVS 2nd Cav Div Inspected C & K Batteries RHA.	
			[illegible] days not specified [illegible] duties were performed.	
			A summary of [illegible] for January is attached.	

2353 Wt. W2544/1454 700,000 5/15 D. D. & L. A.D.S.S./Forms/C. 2118.

Instructions regarding War Diaries and Intelligence Summaries are contained in F. S. Regs., Part II. and the Staff Manual respectively. Title pages will be prepared in manuscript.

WAR DIARY
or
INTELLIGENCE SUMMARY.
(Erase heading not required.)

Army Form C. 2118.

Place	Date	Hour	Summary of Events and Information	Remarks and references to Appendices
			Remaining · Dealt with during · Cured · Evacuated · Died · Discharged · Remaining	
			143 · 640 · 342 · 148 · 2 · 22 · 318	
			[illegible] Maj A.V.C.	
			A.D.V.S. 7th Cav Div	

2353 Wt. W2544/1454 700,000 5/15 D. D. & L. A.D.S.S./Forms/C. 2118.

www.ingramcontent.com/pod-product-compliance
Lightning Source LLC
Chambersburg PA
CBHW081556160426
43191CB00011B/1943
* 9 7 8 1 4 7 4 5 0 1 2 0 0 *